Hugh Latimer

The foremost preacher of the English Reformation

Richard M. Hannula

 **BOOKS**

EP BOOKS
Faverdale North
Darlington
DL3 0PH, England

web: http://www.epbooks.org
e-mail: sales@epbooks.org

EP Books are distributed in the USA by:
JPL Fulfillment
3741 Linden Avenue Southeast
Grand Rapids, MI 49548

e-mail: sales@jplfulfillment.com

First published 2013

British Library Cataloguing in Publication Data available
ISBN: 978-0-85234-930-4

Contents

Introduction

The life of Hugh Latimer (*c.* 1485–1555) spanned the most critical years of the great revival of biblical Christianity known as the Reformation. Within a year of his conversion to Christ in 1524, he became a popular preacher and reformer. He soon fell foul of church authorities who despised his simple gospel message and his condemnation of the church's false doctrines. Of all the English reformers, Latimer was the most effective warrior, doing battle against superstition, the cult of the saints, or any church practice that kept people from looking to Christ alone for salvation. His ministry seesawed between preaching to great crowds in the court chapels of Henry VIII and Edward VI and enduring two stints in dark cells of the Tower of London, and then suffering a martyr's death.

Henry VIII applauded his preaching, and made him a royal chaplain and a bishop; then he imprisoned him and banned him from preaching for eight years. Restored to favour by Edward VI, Latimer often preached before the king and to packed churches throughout the realm. In an age rife with corruption and injustice, his was the strongest and most consistent voice for the poor and dispossessed. He pointed countless of his countrymen to the risen Saviour Jesus Christ. Latimer was widely acclaimed as the foremost preacher of the English Reformation. His sermons still resonate with power and effect nearly 500 years since they were first delivered. 'I have an ear for other preachers,' one nobleman said, 'but I have a heart for Latimer.'

Together with his friend, the Archbishop of Canterbury Thomas Cranmer, Latimer led the fight to make the Scriptures in English legal and accessible to everyone. They laboured for decades to bring the doctrines and practices of the Church of England in line with the Word of God.

The testimony of Latimer's steadfast faith in Christ while being burned at the stake with Nicholas Ridley became one of the most famous martyr stories in the English-speaking world. Hugh Latimer lit a candle for Christ that still shines brightly today. Bishop Ridley called him 'The True Apostle of the English Nation.'

Timeline of Hugh Latimer and the Reformation

1531   Latimer made Parson of West Kington; Bilney burned at the stake

1533   Cranmer installed as Archbishop of Canterbury

1534   Act of Supremacy; English Church severed ties with Rome

1535   Latimer ordained Bishop of Worcester

1536   Preached before Convocation; Calvin's *Institutes* first published

1539   Six Articles enacted; Latimer resigned bishopric; placed under house arrest

1540   Barnes martyred; Latimer released from house arrest; banned from preaching

1546   Latimer imprisoned at the Tower of London; Council of Trent

1547   Henry VIII died; Edward VI crowned; Latimer released from Tower

1549   Act of Uniformity enacted; Use of *Book of Common Prayer* begun

1553   Edward VI died; Mary I crowned; Evangelicals purged; Latimer imprisoned

Hugh Latimer

1554   Latimer condemned as heretic at Oxford; Latin mass re-established

1555   Bradford burned in London; Latimer and Ridley burned at the stake in Oxford

1558   Mary I died; Elizabeth I crowned; English Reformation restored

1
The convert

They only were hearing it said, 'He who used to persecute us is now preaching the faith he once tried to destroy' (Galatians 1:23).

When the earthquake of Martin Luther's (1483–1546) challenge to the Roman church began to rock the foundations of religious life in Europe, leaders of church and state in England feared that their island kingdom would be shaken by the reformation in Germany. They had good reason for concern. The English had long resented papal taxation and the unbridled powers of church courts, where a dungeon cell awaited those who dared bring complaints against the clergy. Money-grubbing and immoral clergymen fuelled an anticlerical bias among the people, who sang ditties featuring 'the dicing and drinking and hunting and wenching' of priests and monks. Cardinal Wolsey (*c.* 1473–1530), the most powerful churchman in the land, alienated the people by using his many church offices to amass unimaginable wealth, which he showed off in the most ostentatious ways possible. He granted his illegitimate son, while he was still a small boy, the benefices of a number of high church offices whose annual revenues were worth a fortune.

Bishops charged for the probate of wills and imposed clerical taxes. Priests demanded fees for everything, including baptism and burial services. 'The priests have no compassion,' a Member of Parliament said. 'The children of the dead should all die of hunger and go begging, rather than the priests should leave them the only cow which the dead man owned.'

'What a trade is that of the priests!' William Tyndale (*c.* 1494–1536), the English reformer, wrote. 'They want money for everything: money for baptisms, for weddings, for buryings, for images, penances, and soul-masses... Poor sheep! The parson shears, the vicar shaves, the parish priest polls, the friar scrapes, the indulgence seller pares... we lack but a butcher to pull off the skin.'

A century and a half earlier, John Wycliffe *(c.* 1329–1384), Master of Balliol College in Oxford, taught that the church's unbiblical doctrines and elaborate rituals hid Christ's gospel from the people. 'Canon Law has no force', Wycliffe wrote, 'when it is opposed to the Word of God.'

At that time, the Latin Vulgate was the only Bible translation sanctioned by the church, but only the educated elite understood Latin. With the help of his students, Wycliffe translated the Bible into English. He sent out his followers to preach and distribute hand-written portions of the English

Scriptures. The Lollards, as they were called, won thousands of Englishmen to Christ, but the bishops convinced the king to crush them. The Lollards were hunted and hounded for decades: scores of them were burned at the stake.

In reaction to Wycliffe's Bible, English authorities enforced severe penalties for translating the Bible into English or reading the Scriptures in English. But persecution by Church and Crown could not fully extinguish the Word of God or Wycliffe's teachings. As late as 1519, seven Lollard parents were burned to death in Coventry for teaching their children the Lord's Prayer and the Ten Commandments in English.

As Luther's books rolled off the printing presses in Germany, they were smuggled into England by seafarers, and then spread throughout the kingdom by merchants and booksellers, many of them Lollards. Opponents of the German Reformation derisively referred to those who embraced it as 'Lutherans'. Others called them 'evangelicals' because of their emphasis on proclaiming the gospel. The Bishop of London warned: 'There have been found certain children of iniquity who are endeavouring to bring into our land the old and accursed Wycliffite heresy, and along with it the Lutheran heresy, foster daughter of Wycliffe's.'

Young King Henry VIII (1491–1547), enraged by Luther's defiance of the pope, called the German reformer 'a serpent, a cunning viper'. He said that Luther's writings 'sprang from the depths of hell'. The well-educated king, with the help of some able bishops, wrote a book attacking Luther's teachings. He relied heavily on the writings of Thomas

Aquinas and other schoolmen, the medieval theologians who created a detailed system integrating Greek philosophy and theology. The pope received Henry's book with delight, proclaiming Henry 'Defender of the Faith'. He needed powerful monarchs to resist the tide of the Reformation. In 1520, King Henry ordered that Luther's writings should be publicly burned in London and in the university towns of Oxford and Cambridge. He made it clear that English supporters of Luther's ideas would face persecution. But book burnings and threats did not stop the ideas of the German Reformation from proliferating.

These ideas found fertile ground at Cambridge University. A revival of classical learning there led many scholars to seek knowledge from original sources. In theology, the schoolmen had relied heavily on allegorical interpretations of the Scriptures; classical scholars sought out the straightforward meaning of biblical texts. This 'New Learning' expanded in Cambridge when Erasmus (c. 1466–1536), the Dutch scholar and theologian, taught there for several years. Erasmus inspired his students to master Greek and to scoff at the abuses of the church. Before he left Cambridge in 1514, some scholars had abandoned the schoolmen and begun to question long-accepted, but corrupt and superstitious, religious practices.

Shortly after leaving Cambridge, Erasmus produced a Greek New Testament compiled from the best sources available. He included with it a lively and more accurate Latin translation. Church leaders in England, fearful that the Greek New Testament might spawn Lutheran ideas, banned the book. Through the providence of God, it was a copy of Erasmus's

New Testament read by a Cambridge scholar which ignited a revival of true faith in Christ that transformed Cambridge University into the hotbed of the Reformation in England.

Despite the ban, Erasmus's New Testament was smuggled into England and sold secretly. Thomas Bilney (c. 1495–1531), a Cambridge student, slipped into the back room of a house and purchased a copy. For years, Bilney had exhausted himself and his money seeking to find peace with God through the guidance of the church. He fasted, disciplined his body, bought pardons, went daily to mass and confessed his sins to priests; but his guilt and despair remained. But as soon as he began to read the Scriptures, God opened his eyes. He discovered a welcoming Saviour, not an aloof judge. Bilney saw that Christ delighted to save sinners. Salvation lay in Christ's hands, not the church's. 'At last I heard Jesus,' Bilney said. 'Christ alone saves his people from their sins. I came to Christ. O mighty power of the Most High! God's instruction and inward working did so exhilarate my despairing heart that my bruised bones leapt for joy.'

A small man with a big heart, Thomas Bilney could not keep the good news to himself. Compelled by the Spirit of God, he followed Christ's call to the healed man: 'Go home to your friends and tell them how much the Lord has done for you, and how he has had mercy on you' (Mark 5:19).

Bilney did not proclaim the good news from the rooftops, but conversation by conversation he urged others to put their faith in Jesus Christ. 'Christ,' he said, 'Christ alone saves his people from their sins.'

Before long, students and lecturers crowded into his study to hear him read and comment on passages from the New Testament. For the first time they saw Christ directly through the Scriptures and not through the eyes of church tradition. Suddenly, Christ was close and personal. They heard the Saviour preaching the good news on the mountainsides of Galilee. They saw him calm the sea, heal the sick, embrace little children, endure the cross and rise triumphant from the tomb. Through it all, they heard Christ calling, 'Come to me, all who labour and are heavy laden, and I will give you rest' (Matthew 11:28).

Many put their trust in the work of the Saviour and not their own works. They rejoiced in a new-found freedom from guilt and sin. This was the beginning of the English Reformation, an awakening of human hearts by the Spirit of God that would spread from Cambridge to every corner of the kingdom.

As Bilney and his friends studied the Scriptures together, they saw the vast chasm that separated the teachings of Christ from the doctrines and practices of the Church of Rome. The church's system of salvation, which emphasized priestly pardons, saints and relics, pilgrimages and ceremonies, seemed very far from the Bible's simple promise: 'Believe in the Lord Jesus, and you will be saved' (Acts 16:31). The proud and pleasure-loving prelates of the English church did not remotely resemble the humble and self-sacrificing Saviour of the Gospels. George Stafford, a university lecturer and friend of Bilney, began expounding the Scriptures to his divinity students without referring to the works of the schoolmen. Many were converted.

Hugh Latimer (*c.* 1485–1555), a priest and a Fellow of Clare Hall, known for his unquestioning loyalty to the Church of Rome and his undying hatred of the Reformation, entered the fray to protect Cambridge students from the heresies of Bilney and Stafford. As more and more students considered evangelical doctrines, Latimer charged them to stick to the traditions of the Roman church. He sought out Stafford's students and railed against their teacher and this new-fangled way of studying the Scriptures. Latimer publicly denounced any instructors who embraced reform. He disrupted their lectures and warned students, 'Do not believe them!'

In the spring of 1524, students and teachers packed Great St Mary's, the university church of Cambridge, to hear Hugh Latimer deliver a theological address. While a Cambridge student, Latimer prepared for the priesthood as men had for 400 years. He wholeheartedly embraced the theology of the schoolmen and the doctrines of the Roman church. When he examined the Scriptures, it was always through the lens of the medieval doctors of the church. He had learned neither Greek nor Hebrew.

The leaders of the colleges appointed him a university preacher, and in 1522 he was chosen to carry the Silver Cross of the university in all official processions, an office given only to men who were zealous in religion and upright in character.

As Latimer spoke to the gathering at Great St Mary's, he lashed out against the German Reformation. With his strong voice, Latimer warned that the Lutheran heresies damned to hell the souls of all who followed them. He scorned the idea that the Bible alone could be the Christian's supreme authority, and charged the audience not to stray from the protective arms of the church.

In the congregation sat Thomas Bilney, then a Fellow of Trinity Hall. As Bilney listened to Latimer's tirade, he sighed and said to himself, 'I was once just like that — full of zeal without knowledge.'

Before the sermon ended, Bilney decided to tell Latimer that sinners could find forgiveness only by trusting Christ. 'But,' he wondered, 'how could I ever get him to listen to me?' It was dangerous to approach Latimer directly; it might lead to arrest as a heretic, but Bilney felt compelled to tell Latimer about Christ's love. Then he hit upon an idea. He walked to Latimer's rooms at Clare Hall and with trembling hand knocked on the door. In a moment, there stood the university cross-bearer. His face was long and thin with a sharp nose. With piercing eyes he stared down at little Bilney. 'Master Latimer,' Bilney said with his head bowed, 'for the sake of God, would you hear my confession?'

Latimer was surprised to see Bilney, for he knew him to be the ringleader of the Cambridge reformers. Latimer assumed that his message at St Mary's must have convinced him of his errors. 'Come in,' he said. Latimer sat down. Bilney knelt on the floor before him and said, 'Let me tell you what happened to my heart; and if I am in error, I am ready to be better instructed.'

'For years,' Bilney told him, 'I did everything in my power to obey the commandments of God and the teachings of the church, but my guilt and sin remained. I went to mass daily and visited priest after priest to confess my sins. I followed their guidance to fast, to hold vigils and to buy pardons until I had no strength left. Nothing relieved me of the sharp sting of my sin. I was a sick and languishing soul.'

Then Bilney told Latimer how he bought a Greek New Testament. 'No sooner had I begun to read it,' he said, 'when I was struck by this sentence of St Paul in 1 Timothy Chapter 1: "Christ Jesus came into the world to save sinners, of whom I am the foremost."'

Bilney explained to Latimer that Paul thought himself the worst of sinners, but he knew he was saved in Christ. Paul believed that Christ had accomplished everything for him through his death on the cross. 'That one sentence from Paul,' Bilney said, his face aglow, 'gave sweet comfort to my soul! My wounded heart, weighed down with guilt, leapt for joy. After this the Scripture became more pleasant to me than honey and the honeycomb. I saw that all my vigils, my fasts, my pilgrimages, my purchase of masses and indulgences were destroying instead of saving me. I looked to Christ and believed that in him I would not perish, but have everlasting life.'

Latimer sat in stunned silence. This heretic was not at all as Latimer had imagined him. He was a devout man who had tried everything the church could offer him to find peace with God. He found forgiveness in Christ by reading the Scriptures and believing them. Although Hugh Latimer did not admit it at the time, he too had an uneasy conscience. His fear of death and damnation had often led him to consider becoming a monk to win God's favour. Latimer had never heard the gospel so simply explained. 'I learned more by hearing his confession', Latimer said later, 'than I had before in many years. From that time onward, I began to smell the Word of God, and forsook the school-doctors and such fooleries'.

Latimer obtained a copy of the New Testament and began to devour it. He saw that it was not what the church did for him or what he did for himself that mattered, but what Christ did for him. Soon he put all his hope of salvation into the hands of his Saviour, Jesus Christ. He was a changed man, a new creation in Christ. Before, he had looked to the church and found fasting, penance, priestly absolution and despair. Now, he looked to Christ and found grace, forgiveness, peace and joy.

Hugh Latimer became Bilney's constant companion. They met for Bible study and prayer. Latimer discovered that Bilney often prayed straight through the night, pleading with God to save sinners. The two walked the countryside around Cambridge and discussed the Scriptures. They frequently walked up Castle Hill, which some students began to refer to as 'Heretic's Hill'. Latimer joined Bilney on his daily outreach into the city. For no sooner had Bilney turned to Christ than he felt compelled to follow in his Saviour's steps by serving others. They brought food to the poor and visited prisoners in jail. They went outside town to the hovels where people suffering from leprosy and other frightening diseases had been banished. While changing their bandages and washing their sores, Bilney and Latimer told them of Christ's love for sinners. Some of these forsaken people believed the good news of Jesus.

Bilney introduced Latimer to the growing circle of awakened Christians at Cambridge who met at The White Horse, an inn near the colleges, to discuss theology and encourage one another in the Lord. Students derisively called the White Horse 'Little Germany', mocking the ideas of Luther that the men embraced.

Soon Latimer, who described his former self as 'the most obstinate papist in England', began to preach in the churches of Cambridge the faith he had once tried to destroy. He surprised his hearers and led many to the Lord. 'Whereas before he was an enemy and almost a persecutor of Christ,' one observer said, 'he now was a zealous seeker after him.'

From the start, Hugh Latimer understood the Bible's most important truth: salvation is a gift of God's free grace through Christ's victory on the cross. He made it the focal point of all his preaching. 'Christ came to deliver us from sin and damnation,' he preached. 'Christ gave his body to be torn upon the cross for that. Neither could any work or law or sacrifice redeem us from that but Christ only.'

Latimer made it clear that Christ's arms were opened wide to welcome even the most vile sinner. 'Though one man had done all the world's sins since Adam's time,' he preached, 'yet he may be remedied by the blood of Jesus Christ; if he believe in him, he shall be cleansed from all his sins. Therefore all our comfort is in him, in his love and kindness. The grace and mercies of God far exceed our sins.'

He made it clear that each man or woman, boy or girl was called to receive the gift of Christ's sacrifice personally by trusting him only for the forgiveness of sins. 'This must be done with constant faith and assured confidence in Christ,' he preached. 'Faith, faith, faith; we are undone for lack of faith.'

It was folly, he said, to trust in one's own good works, or the merits of saints, or pardons from the pope. 'All the passion of all the martyrs that ever were,' he said, 'all the sacrifices of patriarchs that ever were, all the good works that ever were done were not able to remedy our sin, to make satisfaction for our sins, but the blood-shedding of our most merciful Saviour Christ.'

Although Bilney and Latimer continued to attend and lead church services and accepted the core doctrines of the Roman church, their emphasis on Christ's atoning work and the authority of Scripture made enemies among church leaders.

In 1525, West, the Bishop of Ely, heard reports that Latimer was espousing heresy. He decided to drop in unannounced at a church service where Latimer was preaching in the hope of catching him in the act. However, when the bishop entered the church, Latimer stopped speaking. He nodded toward the bishop and said, 'A new audience, especially of such rank, calls for a new message. I will speak of the honourable state of a bishop.'

With no advance preparation, Latimer preached a sermon using Christ as the true model for ministers and bishops to follow. He said that Christ called churchmen to serve humbly and sacrificially, as he did. Clergymen should not seek a life of comfort, but should serve the flock that the

Good Shepherd had entrusted to them. It would not have been difficult for his hearers to recognize how far the English bishops had departed from this teaching. They rarely preached in or visited the churches under their care. They lived in luxury from rich benefices and occupied their time with politics and pleasure.

When the service ended, Bishop West thanked Latimer for his message. 'Indeed,' the bishop said, 'if you will do one thing that I request, I will kneel down and kiss your feet for the good admonition that I have received by your sermon.'

'What do you want me to do for you?' Latimer asked.

'I would like you to preach in this place one sermon against Martin Luther and his doctrine,' Bishop West answered.

Without batting an eye, Latimer replied: 'My Lord, I am not acquainted with the doctrine of Luther, nor are we permitted here to read his works. And therefore it were but a vain thing for me to refute his doctrine, not understanding what he has written, nor what opinion he holds. I am sure that I have preached before you this day no man's doctrine, but only the doctrine of God out of the Scriptures. And if Luther does what I have done, there needs no confutation of his doctrine. Otherwise, when I understand that he does teach against the Scripture, I will be ready with all my heart to confound his doctrine.'

Latimer's answer made the bishop's cheeks flush red. 'Well, well, Mr Latimer,' he snapped, 'I perceive that you somewhat smell of the pan![1] You will repent of this one day.'

Bishop West immediately forbade Latimer to preach anywhere in his diocese or in any of the churches and chapels of Cambridge University. 'Whole swarms of friars and doctors flocked against him on every side,' one man said. Robert Barnes (1495–1540), the prior of Cambridge's Augustinian friary, who had been led to the evangelical faith by Stafford, jumped to Latimer's defence. His monastery was not under the bishop's jurisdiction. Barnes invited Latimer to preach in the monastery's chapel and widely publicized the fact that he would do so. Town and gown of Cambridge prattled about the bishop's effort to suppress Latimer. It appeared that the long-simmering tension between church authorities and the reformers was about to boil over. An overflow crowd packed the chapel to hear Latimer's message at the Christmas Eve service, but it was Barnes himself that caused the greatest stir.

While Latimer spoke in the monastery chapel, Barnes preached at St Edward's, a small church in the heart of Cambridge across from King's College. In the crowded congregation sat several influential opponents of the Reformation. Barnes's blood was up. He launched into an attack on the bishops, calling them followers of Judas and not Christ, accusing them of fleecing their flocks to line their pockets. Cardinal Wolsey got the brunt of it. Barnes decried Wolsey's multiple church offices and his money. He mocked his splendid palaces and regal clothing, his golden shoes and red gloves: 'bloody gloves to keep him warm amidst his ceremonies.'

Outraged university officials brought charges against Barnes, accusing him of slander and heresy. Bilney and Latimer must have wished that Barnes had preached on the grace of Christ and not on the sins of Wolsey. They knew that greater scrutiny and persecution would probably be the result. Still, the friends of the Reformation rushed to Barnes's defence. The controversy agitated and divided the people of Cambridge.

When Wolsey learned of the tumult, he hatched a plot to squelch the evangelical awakening in the city. He ordered the arrest of Barnes and directed agents of the university to make a thorough sweep of the colleges to confiscate banned books. Barnes was seized and carted off to London, but word leaked out about the plan to seize books and the contraband writings were safely hidden away.

Cardinal Wolsey and his advisors examined Robert Barnes and ordered him to acknowledge his heresy and recant. At first Barnes refused, but after several days of threats and incarceration in the notorious Fleet prison, he capitulated. Barnes denied the truth of the gospel to save his life. He would not be the last of the English reformers to do so.

Shortly after Barnes's arrest, Cambridge authorities brought to Wolsey accusations against Bilney and Latimer. They had not directly attacked the cardinal or particular bishops as Barnes had done, so Wolsey was more inclined to be lenient. The cardinal questioned Bilney and released him after he pledged not to preach Lutheran heresies. Then he summoned Hugh Latimer. 'It is reported to me,' Wolsey said, 'that you are much infected with this new fantastical doctrine of Luther and other heretics; that you do very much harm among the youth, and other light-heads, with your doctrine.'

'Your Grace is misinformed,' Latimer said. 'I have studied in my time the ancient doctors of the church and also the school doctors.'

Wolsey told his theologians to ask Latimer questions from the writings of the schoolmen. Latimer demonstrated such a thorough knowledge that Wolsey stopped the interview and said, 'Why do you bring such a man before me into accusation? I had thought that he had been some light-headed fellow that never studied the doctrine of the school doctors. Latimer, tell me why the Bishop of Ely so dislikes your preaching.'

'Not long ago,' Latimer answered, 'I preached before him in Cambridge a sermon wherein I described the office of the bishop, according to the Scripture. Ever after, he could not abide me, but has not only forbidden me to preach in his diocese, but also has inhibited me from preaching in the university.'

After Latimer recounted for Wolsey the particulars of the sermon that he preached before the bishop, Wolsey said, 'If the Bishop of Ely cannot abide such doctrine as you have here repeated, you shall have my licence, and shall preach it unto his beard, let him say what he will.'

Hugh Latimer left London with a licence from Cardinal Wolsey to preach anywhere in England. He returned to Cambridge and preached openly and boldly. His enemies, stymied by Wolsey's support, waited for another opportunity to stop him.

Note
1. A sixteenth-century English idiom meaning to change one's views (usually for the worse).

2

The preacher

How beautiful are the feet of those
who preach the good news!
(Romans 10:15).

In 1527, Thomas Bilney began to leave Cambridge to preach in London and throughout the east of England. He spoke out against the errors of the church that kept people from seeing Christ. 'Let us ask of the Father in the name of the Son,' Bilney preached, 'and he will give unto us. He does not tell us to ask the Father in the name of St Peter or St Paul or other saints, but in *my* name.'

Twice, angry priests seized him while he was speaking, and dragged him from the pulpit. Soon Cardinal Wolsey heard of Bilney's preaching and ordered his arrest. In November 1527, he stood trial before Wolsey and nine bishops at the Chapter House in Westminster Abbey. The great grey arches, high ceiling and massive stone walls of the historic Chapter House dwarfed Bilney as he faced the bishops. They accused him of teaching that people are saved by faith in Christ alone and that Christians should pray to God only and not to saints. They charged him with telling people that it was useless to buy indulgences, go on pilgrimage and light candles before images in church. After a few days of questioning, the bishops declared him a heretic.

However, they did not want to put him to death. They hoped to cripple the Reformation in England by getting Bilney to recant and publicly seek forgiveness for his false teaching as Barnes had done. 'Will you return to the church and revoke your heresies which you have preached?' a bishop asked him.

'I will not be untrue to the gospel,' Bilney said. 'I do not believe that Christ condemns what I have preached.'

Over several days, the bishops pressed him again and again to recant. To persuade him, they had Bilney consult with some of his friends. His friends pleaded with him to recant in order to save his life. Finally, he took their advice and signed a statement that apologized for his teachings.

As penance, the bishops made him carry a faggot, a large bundle of sticks used to fuel the burning of heretics, on his shoulders and walk to St Paul's Cathedral. There they forced him to stand at Paul's Cross holding the faggot while a priest preached a warning against any teachings that were not sanctioned by the church. Afterwards, Wolsey locked Bilney in the Tower of London for a year, and then released him.

Bilney returned to Cambridge a broken man, overwhelmed with sorrow for having denied his faith, believing that he had committed the unpardonable sin. Latimer told him that Christ stood ready to forgive him. 'We stayed with him day and night,' Latimer later said, 'to comfort him as best we could, but he would not receive it. When we quoted comforting passages of Scripture to him, it was as though we were thrusting a sword into his heart. He thought that the whole Scriptures were against him.'

After Bilney had languished for some months in despair, Latimer persuaded him to begin again to study the Scriptures and return to his round of bringing help to the needy. Before long, he felt anew the forgiving grace of God. Full of joy, he shared Christ with students at the university, with prisoners in their cells, and with the infirm on their sick beds. He preached secretly in homes and led Bible studies in his rooms at Trinity Hall.

Meanwhile, the Reformation rapidly gained ground in England through Tyndale's New Testament in English. William Tyndale, a brilliant linguist who had studied at Oxford and Cambridge, came to a living faith in Christ by reading the Greek New Testament. He devoted his life to translating the Bible into simple English so that 'the ploughboy shall know more of the Scriptures than the priests.'

An Act of Parliament prohibited anyone from translating the Scriptures without a bishop's permission, under penalty of death. Tyndale went to the Bishop of London to seek his approval to translate the New Testament into English. When the bishop refused, Tyndale fled to Germany in 1524. There he completed his English translation of the New Testament and had it printed.

By the spring of 1526, thousands of copies of Tyndale's New Testament, hidden in shipments of wheat and linen, had reached the ports of England. Although King Henry condemned the book, and warned merchants and book dealers not to touch it, the New Testament spread across the land. 'I think the Word of God should go forth without persecution; every man within the realm should have it in his mother's tongue,' Latimer said. 'The Word of God is the instrument and fountain of all good things.' One Cambridge student said, 'With manifest authority of God's Word, and arguments invincible, Latimer proved in his sermons that the Holy Scriptures ought to be read in the English tongue by all Christian people.'

The authorities arrested hundreds of people for having the English New Testament, and some died at the stake. But the persecution did not stop the book from being read in humble cottages and great manors, in workshops and monastery cells.

Latimer was coming into his own as an evangelical preacher. He looked to the Saviour as his pattern for ministry. 'Christ is the preacher of all preachers,' Latimer said. More students and townspeople came to hear him; they hung on every word. 'It is all Christ,' Latimer said. 'He humbled himself with all obedience unto death, even to the death of the cross. He took upon himself our sin: to purge it, to cleanse it, to bear the payment of it on his back... Christ would have us to trust in his sacrifice only.' One Cambridge student who later became an evangelical preacher said, 'If I possess the knowledge of God, I owe it, under God, to Latimer.'

Hugh Latimer urged his hearers not to give to Mary and the saints the honour which belonged only to the Lord. 'We have one advocate, not many,' he proclaimed. 'Neither saints, nor anybody else, but only him, and no other, neither by the way of mediation, nor by the way of redemption. He only is sufficient, for he only is all the doer. Let him have all the whole praise!'

He called people to look to Christ alone for salvation, and he called redeemed sinners to live a holy life. These two inseparable truths became the foundation stones of all his sermons. He called it preaching 'true faith and fruits of the same'. Latimer took great pains to separate obedience from any idea of earning salvation, but he felt compelled by the Word of God to proclaim that faith without works is dead. 'Put your faith in Christ,' Latimer said. 'Not a feigned faith without good living, but "faith that works by love". We must do good works, we must endeavour ourselves to live according to the commandments of God; yet, for all that, we must not trust in our good works for that is nothing but a robbing of Christ of his glory and majesty.'

Latimer lived what he preached. As one Cambridge student remarked, 'He watered with good deeds whatever he had said before with godly words.'

He was relentless in his criticism of churchmen who neglected their flocks and obscured the gospel of grace by emphasizing religious duty and not the cross of Christ. Church leaders called him a conceited troublemaker who destroyed the peace and unity of the church. A bishop sent for Latimer and told him that he was shocked that Latimer would not preach the traditions of the church. 'I would be ruled by God's Book,' Latimer answered. 'I would rather be torn by wild horses than dissent one jot from it.'

Congregations found Latimer's sermons gripping. He retold biblical stories with a lively imagination that pulled people into the Scriptures and applied the Word to their hearts. When preaching on Christ's healing of the woman in Luke 8, he said, 'The woman came to him among the press of the people, desiring to touch only the hem of his garment; for she believed that Christ was such a healthful man that she should be sound as soon as she might touch him. All England, yea, all the world, may take this woman for a schoolmistress to learn by her to trust in Christ, and to seek help at his hands.' 'He spoke nothing but left as it were certain pricks or stings in the hearts of the hearers,' one man said of Latimer, 'which moved them to consent to his doctrine.'

To hold a congregation's attention and drive home his points, Latimer used illustrations from everyday life. A few days before Christmas in 1529, he preached his famous sermons 'On the Card' in St Edward's Church in Cambridge. His text came from the passage where the Pharisees asked John the Baptist: 'Who are you?' Latimer told the congregation that that was a question that everyone must ask himself. He said that the honest answer to the question was: 'I am, of myself, … a child of the ire and indignation of God, the true inheritor of hell, a lump of sin.'

But then Latimer told them that Christ had come and taken the penalty of their sin upon himself on the cross. He told them that all who put their trust in Christ could say of themselves: 'I am a Christian man, a Christian woman, a child of everlasting joy through the merits of the bitter passion of Christ.'

Latimer then asserted that every believer must ask a second question of himself: 'What does Christ expect Christians to do?' Pulling from his sleeve a deck of cards, he reminded his hearers that at Christmas time it was customary for families to play card games. 'I intend,' he told them, 'by God's grace, to deal to you Christ's cards, wherein you shall perceive Christ's rule.'

The 'cards' he dealt came from Christ's Sermon on the Mount. The first card was the Lord's teaching that the man who is angry has violated the commandment not to kill. Latimer explained that in order for them to play this card aright, believers needed to understand that Christ's commands were far more demanding than they had ever imagined. After exposing the depths of their sins, he brought them back to the Saviour. 'Wherefore,' he said, 'considering that we are so prone and ready to continue in sin, let us cast down ourselves with Mary Magdalene; and the more we bow down with her towards Christ's feet, the more we shall be afraid to rise again in sin.'

The second 'card' came from Christ's call to love and serve our neighbours. The average churchgoer at this time thought of good works primarily as doing penance, buying indulgences, lighting devotional candles, decorating church statues and going on pilgrimage. He told them that Christ commanded believers to love their neighbours, those created in the image of God, rather than decorating images in church. 'They (the clergy) preach to the people,' Latimer said, 'that dead images ought to be covered with gold, clad with silk garments, laden with precious jewels and lighted with candles, and no cost can be too great. In the meantime, we see Christ's faithful and lively images, bought with his most precious blood, to be hungry, thirsty, cold, and to lie in darkness, wrapped in all wretchedness, yea, to lie there till death take away their miseries.'

Small wonder that many who put their trust in Christ through Latimer's preaching began to spend their time as he and Bilney did, caring for the sick and feeding the hungry. 'Oh how vehement was he in rebuking all sins,' one Cambridge student said of him. 'How sweet and pleasant were his words exhorting unto virtue! He spoke against the reposing our hope in our own works, or in other men's merits.'

The 'Sermons on the Card' ignited a fierce controversy in Cambridge. Defenders of church traditions resented his slighting of ceremonial practices. Buckenham, the prior of Blackfriars, preached a sermon attacking Latimer's teaching. He took particular aim at Latimer's call for the Scriptures to be available to everyone in English. He argued that the common people could not understand the Scriptures for themselves and that danger lurked within its figurative language. 'Thus,' the prior said, 'when the simple man reads the words, "If your eye offends you, pluck it out, and cast it from you," he will pluck out his eyes, and so the whole realm will be full of blind men. And thus by the reading of Holy Scripture will the whole kingdom come into confusion.'

Latimer responded to Buckenham's message with a sermon in which he argued that people had enough sense to understand the use of figures of speech and metaphors, for they encountered them every day. As Latimer preached, Friar Buckenham sat in the congregation dressed in his black-hooded robe. Latimer said that if the people saw a painting of a fox wearing a friar's hood and preaching, they would understand its meaning. 'There is none so mad,' Latimer said, 'to take this to be a fox that preaches, but know well enough the meaning of the matter, which is to point out to us, what hypocrisy, craft, and subtle dissimulation lies hidden many times in these friar's hoods, showing us thereby to beware of them.'

The heads of several colleges preached against Latimer's doctrine and complained about him to university officials. The contest in the pulpits of Cambridge grew so tense that a representative of Henry VIII wrote to the vice-chancellor of Cambridge University directing him to put a stop to the rancour.

King Henry was aware of Latimer for more than just his preaching. At this time, Henry wanted to divorce his wife, Catherine of Aragon (1485–1536), daughter of the wealthy monarch of Spain. She had been married to his older brother Arthur for a few months before Arthur died at the age of fifteen. Henry's father, King Henry VII, wanted to keep Catherine and her rich dowry in England. He arranged for Catherine to marry his second son, Prince Henry, when he came of age. It was a violation of church law to marry the wife of one's brother. It took a special dispensation from the pope to clear the way for Prince Henry to marry his brother's widow. When Henry VII died, Prince Henry was crowned King Henry VIII. He and Catherine were married shortly thereafter.

Catherine suffered several stillbirths and miscarriages, but eventually gave birth to a daughter. Over time, Henry came to believe that the pregnancies ending in death and the lack of a male heir demonstrated that the marriage displeased God. He surmised that it was God's judgement for violating the Bible's prohibitions in Leviticus against marrying a brother's wife. He asked the pope to annul the marriage, but that proved difficult for the pope to do. Catherine's nephew, Charles V (1500–1558), who was the King of Spain and the Holy Roman Emperor, opposed the annulment. His troops controlled Italy and he held the pope as a virtual prisoner. The pope did not want to anger Charles or Henry, so he stalled for time.

For several years, the pope dragged out the process of investigating the annulment request. In the meantime, Henry took a fancy to Anne Boleyn (c. 1501–1536) and wanted to marry her. In 1529, Thomas Cranmer (1489–1556), an evangelical Cambridge scholar, suggested to the king's ministers that Henry bypass the pope altogether and submit the question of annulling his marriage to university theologians. Henry jumped at the opportunity. The king found that many of the English scholars who supported the Reformation also supported the annulment. Latimer took the king's side in the matter.

In 1530, the king ordered Cambridge University to form a committee to determine whether his marriage was forbidden by the Word of God. Latimer and several other evangelicals, including his friend Edward Crome, were selected to serve on the committee, as were a number of staunch supporters of the Roman church. Henry cajoled and intimidated to get the decision he wanted from them. The king heard that Latimer had argued forcefully for the annulment.

In the spring of 1530, Henry invited Latimer to preach before the royal court at Windsor during Lent. Before Latimer gave his first sermon at court, an influential official pulled him aside and advised, 'You must beware, whatever you do, do not speak contrary to the king's wishes; let him have his sayings; follow him; go with him.'

Latimer had no intention of following the advice. He held back nothing in his sermon before the king, and Henry asked him to continue preaching through Easter. The vice-chancellor of Cambridge, who had visited the royal court, wrote: 'The king greatly praised Mr Latimer's sermon ... Mr Latimer preaches still, to the great annoyance of his opponents.'

Latimer exposed sin and exalted Christ. 'Sin must be revealed,' he declared. 'Sin must be plainly spoken against.' In a sermon preached before the king, Latimer said, 'God is great, eternal, almighty, everlasting; and the Scripture, because of him, is also great, eternal, most mighty, and holy ... there is no king, emperor, magistrate, or ruler, but is bound to give credence unto God's Holy Word.'

Despite Henry's many faults, he admired Latimer for his boldness in declaring the unvarnished truth. Once Latimer had told the king, 'You have the corrupt nature of Adam in you ... so you have no less need of the merits of Christ's passion for your salvation, than I and other of your subjects have.' He told Henry, who was so proud to be called 'Defender of the Faith', that God did not need 'a defender of his faith: for he will not have it defended by man or by man's power, but by his Word only'.

Once after Latimer had preached at court, one courtier asked another, 'How do you like the preacher?'

'Even as I like him always', the man replied. 'A seditious fellow!'

'Yet I comfort myself with this', Latimer said, 'that Christ himself was noted to be a stirrer up of the people against the emperor; and was contented to be called seditious.'

His preaching included illustrations from his own experiences, everyday life and current events, but his sermons were grounded in and saturated with Scripture. In one sermon that he preached before the king, Latimer referenced Paul's advice to Timothy, the Beatitudes from Christ's Sermon on the Mount, the command to obey God from Deuteronomy 1, the wisdom of Solomon, Isaiah's prophecies against unrighteous judges, King David and Absalom's rebellion, Christ's temptation in the wilderness, Jeremiah on the hardness of the heart, Paul on justification, Christ in the Garden of Gethsemane, the destruction of Sodom and Gomorrah, Lot's wife, the complacency of the people before the Great Flood and Christ's sacrifice on the cross.

Meanwhile, the delaying tactics of the pope in Rome infuriated King Henry VIII and led directly to the downfall of Cardinal Wolsey, the papal legate. Henry stripped Wolsey of his role as Chancellor of England, and he surrendered most of his wealth to the king.

As Henry challenged the power of the pope in England, he made it clear that he was not in favour of the reformers' doctrine. He wanted a church independent of Rome's authority, but based on the beliefs and ceremonies of the Roman church. The king replaced Wolsey as Chancellor with Thomas More (1478–1535), a fierce opponent of the Reformation who was more willing to shed blood to crush it than Wolsey had been. Henry ordered the bishops to redouble their efforts to root out heretics and bring them to trial.

But the king was not unalterably opposed to all of the teachings of the evangelicals. He had told the Imperial ambassador, 'Luther had evidently mixed up a good deal of heresy in his books, but that was not a sufficient reason for rejecting the many truths he brought to light.' Henry wrote to the heads of Cambridge and Oxford universities and asked them to send scholars to London to examine Tyndale's English New Testament and the contents of religious books by Tyndale and others. Latimer and his fellow reformer, Edward Crome, were two of the twelve delegates sent from Cambridge, but a majority of the scholars at the conference opposed the Reformation. The reformers stood little chance of swaying them. After two weeks of discussion, the conference presented its findings to the king at Westminster Palace. They declared that Tyndale's Bible in English contained 'corrupt doctrine and pernicious heresies'. They took great umbrage at the marginal notes that Tyndale had included, which promoted evangelical doctrines. They also condemned the books of Tyndale and other reformers.

The reformers told the king that there was a great need for the people of England to have the Bible in their own language. Since Tyndale's Bible was unacceptable, another translation should be commissioned at once. Before the king dismissed the conference in the spring of 1530, he promised that he would 'cause the New Testament to be faithfully and purely translated into the English tongue that it might be freely given to the people ... if it shall then seem convenient to his Grace'. Unfortunately, it would be several years before 'it seemed convenient' to Henry to allow the Bible in English in his realm.

Despite their different views, Henry liked Latimer and made him a royal chaplain. Latimer spent time preaching at court and proclaiming the good news of Christ from pulpits in London. When it became clear to Latimer that Henry was stalling on his pledge to permit an English translation of the Scriptures, he wrote the king a long and impassioned letter urging him to fulfil his promise.

Latimer wrote that he trembled to bring the matter before him. 'But if I do not proclaim what I have read and learned in the Bible, I would provoke the wrath of God'. He warned the king that those who advised him to forbid the use of the English Scriptures were hiding the truth and the light of the gospel. 'They go about to stop it and hinder it, saying that the Holy Scriptures should not be read in our mother

tongue, saying that it would cause heresy and insurrection
... but others have shown your Grace how necessary it is to
have the Scriptures in English.'

He reminded the king of his promise to support a
translation of the English Bible and challenged him to fulfil
it immediately. 'Today, not tomorrow,' Latimer wrote.

In spite of fierce opposition, the Reformation was gaining
ground in Britain. A growing number of noblemen no longer
bequeathed money to the church for masses to be said for
their souls in purgatory. Some men included in their wills a
testimony of their faith in Christ, abandoning the traditional
form which included statements about the Virgin Mary and
the saints. When William Tracy, an evangelical justice of
the peace, died in 1531, his will stated that he trusted his
salvation to the merits of Christ alone, rejecting the works of
men and masses for the dead. When the will became known,
Archbishop Warham declared Tracy a heretic and ordered
that his corpse be dug up from the consecrated ground of the
churchyard where he was buried. His body was disinterred
and burned.

Latimer soon grew weary of the royal court. He asked to
be assigned to a country church where he could use his
gifts and feel at home. In January 1531, he became rector
of West Kington, a rural parish in the west of England near
Bristol.

Meanwhile, alarmed at the spread of the evangelical
faith, Chancellor More sought to cut it out of the English
church like a cancer. 'Numbers of Englishmen,' More said,

'who would not a few years ago even hear Luther's name mentioned are now publishing his praises! England is now like the sea which swells and heaves before a great storm.'

While Latimer began his ministry at West Kington, Thomas Bilney decided to launch out from Cambridge to preach the good news of Jesus which he had denied before the bishops four years earlier. Late one evening, he told his friends, 'I am going up to Jerusalem.' They knew that he meant that he was no longer going to serve the Lord quietly in Cambridge, and that arrest and execution awaited him.

Bilney preached in houses, barns and fields. He preached throughout his home county of Norfolk. 'Leave your idolatry to saints,' he proclaimed. 'Our Saviour Christ is our mediator between us and the Father.' He told his hearers that he had recanted out of cowardice and all that he had preached formerly was true. Wherever he went he gave away copies of Tyndale's English New Testament.

In Norwich, Bilney led a woman to Christ. When he brought her the New Testament, officers sent from the bishop arrested him and threw him into prison. Nix, the blind bishop of Norwich, was a notorious enemy of the Reformation. He moved quickly to execute the relapsed heretic. Nix sent a courier to Thomas More to obtain written permission to burn Bilney. 'Go your way and burn him first,' the Lord Chancellor told him, 'and then afterwards come to me for a bill.' Friars and church officials badgered Bilney to recant, but this time his faith in God was unshakeable. The bishop handed him over to the sheriff for execution.

During Bilney's trial, Latimer travelled to London. He preached a sermon in which he admonished judges to rule fairly and not to accept false reports made against the accused. He said that if the Bishop of London had accepted the accusations of the enemies of St Paul, 'then good St Paul must have borne a faggot on his back at Paul's Cross'.

Enraged when he learned of Latimer's remarks, the Bishop of London complained to Henry VIII. He accused Latimer of defending Bilney, undermining church authority and promoting heresy. Latimer wrote to a friend: 'I have known Bilney a great while, I think much better than ever did the Bishop of London ... I have known few so prompt and ready to do every man good after his power ... I cannot but wonder, if a man living so mercifully, so charitably, so patiently, so confidently, so studiously and virtuously shall die an evil death, what shall become of me, such a wretch as I am?'

On the night before Bilney was to be burned to death, Cambridge friends came to visit him. One of them remarked that he was surprised to see him so cheerful and happy. 'Well,' Bilney said, 'I will soon have unspeakable joy in heaven.' He told them that he found great comfort in Isaiah, chapter 43: 'Fear not: for I have redeemed you; I have called you by name, you are mine. When you pass through the waters, I will be with you; and through the rivers, they shall not overwhelm you; when you walk through fire, you shall not be burned ... For I am the LORD your God, the Holy One of Israel, your Saviour.'

The next morning armed guards marched him outside the city to a low valley known as the Lollards' Pit. A crowd of spectators had gathered to watch him burn. 'Good people,' Bilney said, 'I have come here to die. But so you might know that I leave this present life as a true Christian man in a right belief towards Almighty God, I will tell you what I believe.'

Lifting up his hands, he said the *Apostles' Creed*. Then he knelt, prayed and recited Psalm 143. When he stood up, the executioner tied him to the stake and lit the fire. Bilney called out 'Jesus, I believe.' So died Thomas Bilney, the first evangelist of the English Reformation.

Latimer mourned for his friend, and wondered whether he would one day suffer the same fate. Long after his friend's death, Latimer said, 'Bilney was God's instrument to call me to know Him. I thank Bilney next to God for the knowledge that I have in the Word of God. Little Bilney, that blessed martyr of God.'

3

The parson

He said to him, 'Feed my lambs'
(John 21:15).

When Latimer took up residence in the rectory in West Kington it must have brought back memories of his childhood. The ploughed fields and the pastureland with grazing sheep and cows were familiar sights to him. His new home sat near the old Roman Fosse Way which cut its straight path across England. One hundred and twenty miles to the north-east it passed by the rented farm near Leicester where Latimer had spent his boyhood.

In his small parish he was responsible for a few hundred souls; he called it 'My little cure'. As always, he implored his flock to put their faith in the mercies of Christ and his finished work on the cross. 'Begin with Christ, learn to know Christ and why he came, namely that he might save sinners,' he preached. 'He is our comfort, it is the majesty of Christ and his blood shedding that cleanses us from our sins. Such a friend is our Saviour! How inestimably are we bound to him! What thanks ought we to give him for it!'

As the son of a yeoman farmer from a small village in central England, Latimer understood the dignity and drudgery of the life of the common man. Poor country folk as much as university scholars or the ruling elite were created in God's image and worthy of respect. 'The poorest ploughman is in Christ equal with the greatest prince,' he said.

He taught that all vocations were honourable before the Lord. 'Our Saviour Christ,' Latimer said, 'before he began his preaching, was a carpenter and he got his living with great labour. Therefore let no man disdain to follow him in a common calling and occupation. For as he blessed our nature by becoming man, so in his doing, he blessed all occupations and arts.'

As he had at Cambridge and at court, he preached true faith and its fruits. Latimer knew that Christ did not come to live, die and rise again merely to proclaim truth, but to bring life, abundant life, eternal life. He taught that believers were born again to new life lived by grace in the Spirit, a life of trust, gratitude and obedience. One biographer summed up Latimer's ministry well: 'To him the Reformation was not so much the revival of old scriptural truth long concealed, as the restoration of an old scriptural life that had been almost totally obscured by ceremonies and ecclesiastical superstitions.'

He strove to pull his people out of their spiritual complacency by disabusing them of the widely-held belief that they would be saved in the end because they had been baptized. 'Men who despise God', Latimer said, 'call out: "We are baptized, therefore we are saved." Make no mistake; to be baptized and not obey God's commandments is to be worse than the Turks and the heathens. Regeneration comes from the Word of God; it is by hearing and believing this Word that we are born again.'

As he challenged them in Christ to put sin to death and put on good works, he urged them to pray for the grace to do it. 'Therefore let us endeavour ourselves to do his will and pleasure and when we are not able to do it, as we are not indeed, let us call on him for help,' Latimer said. 'This I would have you to consider, that every morning when you rise from your bed, you would say these words with a faithful heart and earnest mind: "Lord, rule and govern me, so order my ways so that sin get not the victory of me, that sin rule me not; but let thy Holy Spirit inhabit my heart."'

At another time he said, 'We must pray at all times without intermission. When we go to bed, when we rise in the morning, when we go about our business, or when we are on horseback, ever pray.'

Latimer insisted that his congregation pray to God alone, not to saints. He told them that prayer must be offered to God the Father by faith in Christ with heart and mind engaged. To a people who had been taught that an acceptable form of prayer was to rattle off ten or twenty 'Ave Marias' in a row, Latimer's teaching was astounding. 'Invoke the Father of heaven, trusting in Christ's merits,' Latimer preached. 'Whoever resorts to God without Christ, he resorts in vain.'

Back in London, King Henry seized control of the English church. In January 1531, Thomas Cromwell, a member of the Privy Council, burst into a meeting of Convocation, the body of bishops and deans who controlled the church. Cromwell told them that they were duty bound to submit to the authority of the king, but their sworn allegiance to the pope undermined their loyalty to the Crown. He informed the startled bishops that they were in violation of English law and that they faced imprisonment if they failed to sever their ties with Rome.

Having seen the fall of Cardinal Wolsey, the bishops knew that the king would have his way. In short order, the bishops begged the king's forgiveness and paid the royal treasury a huge fine. Before Henry would grant them his pardon, he required them to pledge their loyalty to him as 'protector and supreme head of the church and clergy in England'. The bishops complained about the king's usurpation of church authority, but they soon submitted to Henry. 'They have declared him the pope of England,' the Spanish ambassador reported.

The conservative bishops and the public at large had no love for the pope. Years of Roman pontiffs' pomp, immorality and lust for power had seen to that. They were willing to submit to royal supremacy of the church as long as the beliefs and practices of the church remained unchanged. Meanwhile, Stokesley, the Bishop of London, brought heresy charges against Latimer for the sermon he had preached in London a few months earlier. He said that he would not tolerate Latimer's 'fraudulent and pestiferous preaching, whereby he corrupts the people, and seduces them from the received doctrine of the church'.

Stokesley summoned Latimer to appear before him at St Paul's Cathedral on 29 January 1532. Latimer protested that he was not under the jurisdiction of the Bishop of London. He complained that he was suffering from severe headaches and that a long journey in the 'dead of winter' would put great strains on his body; but all to no avail. 'What a world is this,' Latimer wrote to a friend, 'that I shall be put to so great labour and pains for preaching a poor simple sermon.'

For six weeks he faced interrogation by Bishop Stokesley and his agents. Then Stokesley brought heresy charges against him to Convocation, presided over by Warham, the Archbishop of Canterbury. Latimer stood trial before the bishops in the Chapter House at Westminster Abbey, the same place where Bilney had recanted five years earlier. The bishops demanded that Latimer affirm the existence of purgatory, prayer to the saints in heaven, the value of pilgrimages and decorating church statues. When Latimer refused, the archbishop excommunicated him and placed him under arrest.

'I stand fixed on the side of the commandments of God,' Latimer told the archbishop, 'and as long as life shall be permitted to me, I will continue.'

But Convocation was relentless. For nearly three months, bishops and theologians hounded him to submit. For a time Latimer stood firm, informing them, 'Christ has ordered us to preach not all things which you choose to esteem necessary, but those things which He has commanded... There are occasions on which one must obey God rather than man.'

In a final effort to win release, Latimer appealed directly to the king. It is likely that Henry counselled him to admit errors. In the end, he succumbed to the pressure. On bended knee, he confessed that he had erred in discretion and doctrine. 'I ask forgiveness for my misbehaviour,' he said.

The king told the bishops to restore Latimer to his office. Before he returned to West Kington, some friends of James Bainham, a condemned heretic, asked Latimer to visit him in prison. Bainham was to be burned at the stake the next day. Bishop Stokesley's court had condemned him for possessing the New Testament in English and for advocating evangelical teaching. During his trial he had said, 'I know no man to have preached the Word of God sincerely and purely, and true to Scripture, except Master Crome and Master Latimer.'

Upon entering his prison cell, Latimer asked Bainham the grounds on which he was being put to death. He warned him that a man should not suffer execution willingly unless in a good cause for the honour of God. Bainham told Latimer, 'I spoke against purgatory, that there was no such thing; but it picked men's purses.' He said that he believed that masses for the dead were worthless, as were prayers to saints. All of which, he told Latimer, 'I defended by the authority of the Scriptures.'

Latimer told him not to recant against his conscience or the Scriptures. Since the government confiscated the property of heretics, Bainham worried about his family's survival. Latimer assured him that he could trust in the goodness of God for the safekeeping of his wife and children. Bainham warmly thanked him and said, 'I likewise do exhort you to stand to the defence of the truth; for you that shall be left behind have need of comfort.'

Latimer returned to West Kington determined to re-examine the Scriptures regarding purgatory and other doctrines and practices.

By the time that Latimer arrived back at his rectory, he had been away for four months. Things had not changed much in his rural parish, but great changes were taking place in church and state in London. Thomas More, Henry VIII's Chancellor, resigned his post rather than accept Henry's claim to be the supreme head of the church. Henry had More beheaded. In his place, he appointed Thomas Cromwell. Cromwell used his office to advance the evangelical faith.

At about the same time, the Archbishop of Canterbury died. Much to the chagrin of Convocation, the king appointed the Cambridge reformer, Thomas Cranmer, to replace him. Henry chose Cranmer because he had been the leading defender of his divorce. One reformer said of Cranmer, 'He is in a perilous place, but yet in a glorious place to plant the gospel.'

Suddenly, Latimer and other supporters of the Reformation had an ally as the king's first minister and a friend as the most powerful churchman in the land. Cranmer's first official acts as archbishop were to approve Henry's annulment and his new marriage to Anne Boleyn.

If the bishops thought that they had heard the last of Latimer, they were wrong. As Latimer began to preach again in his parish and the surrounding towns, he stirred up controversy. At times, his passion got the better of him. He could be cutting, rash and injudicious in his choice of words when preaching. He admitted to Convocation, 'I have spoken indiscreetly in the vehemence of speaking.' He told others that at times he spoke 'somewhat discourteously'.

A conservative priest rebuked Latimer for the reports he had received of a sermon Latimer preached in a nearby town. 'You declared that all bishops, popes, and rectors (except yourself and some more of your class, I suppose) were thieves and robbers, and that all the rope in England would not suffice to hang them.'

In response, Latimer protested that he did not say all popes, bishops and rectors were thieves and robbers, but only those who did not enter by the door of Christ. However, Latimer did not deny his reference to the rope for hanging them.

In the spring of 1533, he was invited to preach in Bristol, the commercial centre of western England. Huge crowds came out to hear him. There were many Lollards in the city who were anxious to hear him preach, and many supporters of the Roman church ready to condemn him.

In a city famous for its devotion to the Virgin Mary, he told them to stop looking to Mary 'as though she had not been saved by Christ, a whole Saviour both of her and all who are and shall be saved'.

He told them that providing for their families, paying their debts, and caring for their poor neighbours was far better for their souls and a wiser use of their resources than going on pilgrimage or decorating images. As for purgatory, he preached that it was a doctrine abused by the church for financial gain. 'There are but two states,' Latimer would later say, 'the state of salvation and the state of damnation.'

The city was deeply divided over his preaching. Those who had despaired of ever finding peace with God through the church's system of works and rituals rejoiced to hear of a welcoming Saviour. Others, outraged by his attack on practices upon which they had pinned their hopes of salvation, protested loudly. Latimer returned to his parish, but the storm in Bristol raged on.

In every corner of the city people hotly debated the teachings of the reformer. Fist fights ensued and a riot broke out. Slanderous lyrics against Latimer circulated through Bristol. An acrostic poem attacking Latimer was tacked to a church door:

> L   for Lollard stands in this place.
> A   for an error of great iniquity.
> T   for traitor to God, lacking grace.
> I   for ignorance of the true Trinity.
> M   for maintainer of those that nought be.
> E   for 'eretic, as learned men saith.
> R   for rebeller against Christ's faith.

A formal protest from a churchman in Bristol reached Convocation in London, complaining that Latimer spoke against pilgrimages and worshipping saints and taught that Mary, the mother of Jesus, was a sinner in need of Christ's grace. Convocation, angry at Latimer's failure to abide by his pledge of submission, sent an order to Bristol forbidding him from preaching there without the permission of the bishop of the diocese.

While Latimer was silenced, his critics were not. Priests and monks took to the pulpits attacking his doctrines and his character. They sought feebly to defend traditional church practices from the Bible. One clergyman supported pilgrimages from Christ's promise to reward a hundredfold everyone who left his family to follow him. 'Whoever went on pilgrimage', he said, 'left his father and mother and brethren for the time that he was away from home; therefore our Lord's promise applied to him. Therefore, let him put in the box at the shrine of the saint, whatever he will, he shall have a hundred times as much here in this world, and in the world to come everlasting life!'

Latimer wrote letters to defend his preaching regarding purgatory, pilgrimages, and the intercession of the saints. 'As touching the saints in heaven,' Latimer wrote, 'they are not our mediators by way of redemption; Christ alone is our Mediator and theirs both. The blood of martyrs has nothing to do by way of redemption; the blood of Christ is enough for a thousand worlds.'

He complained that his critics, although quick to slander him, were unwilling to debate him openly. However, one of his opponents, John Hilsey, Prior of the Blackfriars, did meet with Latimer and discuss his preaching. Afterwards Hilsey, convinced by the biblical support for Latimer's beliefs, became his friend and a fellow reformer.

Because of the uproar in Bristol, Latimer and his doctrine were discussed by noblemen and peasants across England. Many of Latimer's critics in Bristol were also opponents of the king's claim to be the supreme head of the church. Some of them spoke out against the king's remarriage. Cromwell sent a commission to investigate the troubles over Latimer's preaching. The end result was that all of Latimer's opponents were disgraced and a few were imprisoned. Archbishop Cranmer granted Latimer a licence to preach. But Latimer expected further persecution from the clergy, who fought to maintain their power and comfortable livings. 'This is the wasp that stings them,' he said, 'and makes them swell.'

In the meantime, Latimer poured his energy into the work of his parish, preaching several times a week, visiting the sick and counselling the troubled. His heart ached for the common people to be free in Christ, released from the shackles of superstition and dead works. Latimer refuted the old faith, which placed such emphasis on 'holy water, bells, palms, candles, ashes, and what not! And of these things every one has taken away some part of Christ's sanctification; every one has robbed some part of Christ's passion and cross.'

He told the story of visiting a dying relative shortly after Latimer had earned his university degree and become a priest. Not long after he entered the sick man's house, the man died. An older cousin of Latimer's wanted him to ward off the devil by making certain signs of the cross with a lighted candle over the dead man's body. Latimer made an attempt, but being unfamiliar with the ritual, he failed to satisfy the old woman. She snatched the candle from his hand, saying, 'It's a pity that your father wasted so much money on you.'

From Latimer's rectory he watched the multitudes on pilgrimage. 'You would wonder', he wrote, 'to see how they come by flocks out of the West Country to many images, but chiefly to the Blood of Hailes.' The Blood of Hailes was the treasured relic of Hailes Abbey, a monastery near Worcester. In 1270, a nobleman presented the Abbey with a vial purported to contain blood shed by Christ on the cross. It came with the seal of authenticity from the Patriarch of Jerusalem. Stories of miracles associated with the relic abounded. Many pilgrims believed that the sight of it brought them eternal life. Over the centuries, popes had granted indulgences to those who venerated the relic of the 'Holy Blood of Hailes'. Pope Eugenius promised absolution to all 'who give anything to the worship of God and that precious blood'.

Latimer preached against the superstition surrounding the Blood of Hailes and other famous shrines in England. 'I read in Scripture: "We, being justified by faith, have peace with God." If I see the blood of Christ with the eye of my soul, that is true faith that his blood was shed for me... but I do not read that I have peace with God, or that I am translated from death to life, because I see with my bodily eye the Blood of Hailes.' When, in 1538, Henry VIII ordered the destruction of all pilgrimage shrines in England, the Blood of Hailes was brought to London for inspection. The King's Council declared it to be 'clarified honey and coloured with saffron'.

Henry realized that Latimer's preaching gifts could be used to break the people's centuries-old loyalty to the pope. In the summer of 1534, the king sent Latimer on a preaching tour. In Exeter, he preached in Greyfriars' churchyard, and despite the rain the large crowd stayed to listen. While the infuriated friars banned him from preaching again in their grounds, the warden of the abbey was won over to the gospel of Christ. Latimer then preached in a parish church, where the people so jammed the sanctuary that the overflow crowd outside broke the church windows in order to hear him. In the middle of the sermon, as the congregation listened with rapt attention, a nobleman strode up to the pulpit shouting, 'Silence, you heretic knave! Come down from that pulpit or, by God, I will pull you down by the ears myself.'

The shocked audience wondered what Latimer would do. He ignored the enraged man standing before him and finished his sermon. His composure impressed his hearers. Latimer's preaching bore fruit. Priors and friars and clerks and ploughmen turned from their efforts to win God's favour through religious duties and found forgiveness in Christ.

In November 1534, Parliament passed the Act of Supremacy, which declared the king 'the only supreme head on earth of the Church of England.' Subjects who refused to acknowledge the king's role in the church were guilty of high treason. Henry now had full authority to reform doctrine and oversee the bishops. It became illegal for English clergy or citizens to seek consecration to office from the pope. Bishops would be selected by the king's recommendation. All payments of any kind to Rome ceased. Before this time, the English bishops had to give their first year's salary to the pope, as well as annual financial gifts. If the English prelates thought they were off the hook for paying the fees in the future, they were sadly mistaken. Henry made them pay even higher amounts to the royal treasury.

Although the king and Parliament abolished the authority of the pope in England, they had no intention of adopting the central teachings of the reformers. Apart from Cromwell and Cranmer, no one else in high office favoured a thorough reformation of the doctrines and practices of the English church. In December 1534, under the urging of Convocation, Henry issued a decree banning evangelical books and any English translation of the Bible not approved by the king. Anyone who challenged the accepted teachings of the church could be burned at the stake for heresy. The king then ordered the execution of several supporters of papal supremacy and had fourteen Anabaptists burned for heresy. His agents continued to hunt for William Tyndale on the Continent.

Meanwhile, the king set his sights on the absentee foreign bishops who collected the rich livings of a bishopric but never resided in England. Cromwell and Cranmer used their influence with Henry to put reformers in their place. They wanted Latimer's strong voice in an influential position to advance the Reformation. In 1535, Henry removed the Italian prelate who had been the Bishop of Worcester and appointed Latimer to replace him.

4

The bishop

'I will also speak of your testimonies before kings and shall
not be put to shame'
(Psalm 119:46).

Latimer, now in his early fifties, poured his energies into his bishopric. His circumstances had changed dramatically. He had the use of several country estates and Hartlebury Castle as his home in Worcester. The pomp and wealth did not interest him. The power to influence preaching in his diocese and the kingdom did. For most Englishmen, their bishop was a legal officer to be feared. They were grateful that they rarely, if ever, saw him. Latimer had no intention of being a typical bishop.

He embarked upon a thorough visitation of his far-flung diocese, riding through wind and rain on poor roads that were often clogged with mud. Latimer discovered that centuries of spiritual neglect had fostered corruption and superstition in every corner. People and priests alike prayed more to the saints than to the Saviour. They believed that holy water could ward off the devil and the ringing of bells could protect from disaster. They thought that an annual pilgrimage to a shrine honouring Mary would bring financial blessing.

Some churches had not had a parson in decades. Latimer found that most of the priests did not understand the gospel, nor could they recite the Lord's Prayer or the Ten Commandments. He directed the priests to memorize the Lord's Prayer and the Ten Commandments and the *Apostles' Creed* in English. If they were capable of reading Latin, he instructed them to read and study the Bible.

Using the money at his disposal, he set an example of bringing relief to the poor. He taught the people how to think about the resources that God gave them. 'They are ours,' Latimer said, 'upon the condition that we spend them to the honour of God, and the relieving of our neighbours.'

Latimer believed that bishops should be busy preaching God's Word and not simply serving as administrators. He ended each sermon by reciting the Lord's Prayer in English. He encouraged the people to say it together with him to help them learn it. 'Truly it is the greatest comfort in the world to talk with God and to call upon him in this prayer that Christ himself has taught us,' Latimer said.

The people of Latimer's diocese had never had a bishop who preached. For forty years, their bishops had been foreign prelates who collected their salaries and lived permanently in Italy. Once, while travelling through his diocese, Latimer sent word ahead into a town that he would preach there the following day. When he arrived, he found the church locked and scarcely a person in town. Finally, a parishioner approached him and said, 'Sir, this is a busy day for us. We cannot hear you. This is Robin Hood's Day and the parish is gone abroad to gather for Robin Hood.'

'It is no laughing matter, my friends,' Latimer said later in a sermon. 'It is a weeping matter, under the pretence for gathering for Robin Hood, a traitor and a thief, to put out a preacher ... to prefer Robin Hood to God's Word.'

Latimer insisted that the clergymen under his authority preach the Word of God faithfully and clearly. He tried to rid his diocese of priests who were unwilling to proclaim the truths of Scripture. When vacancies occurred in churches, he chose reform-minded preachers to fill them. He knew that the Lord demanded bold men to preach the gospel: 'Men of activity that have stomachs to do their office,' Latimer said, 'not milksops and white-livered knights. They must wise, hearty, and hardy.'

A growing number of young evangelists inspired by Latimer and other reformers were preaching the gospel throughout the kingdom. Latimer told preachers to proclaim not just their favourite passages of Scripture, but the whole counsel of God. Latimer said, 'Christ says, "Go and teach all things." All what things? "All," Christ says, "which I have commanded you." Christ does not say all which you yourselves may choose to account necessary for preaching. Let us so exert ourselves with one accord to preach the doctrines of God.'

Many of the priests and laymen opposed him, calling him a 'heretic' and a 'Lollard whore's son'. One churchman in Bristol said that Latimer was 'a false harlot in his preaching'. Another said, 'I wish he had never been born. I trust to see him burned ere I die!' 'We must be content to be despised with Christ here in this world,' Latimer said, 'that we may be glorified with him in yonder world.'

As Latimer became known by the people of his diocese, they came out in growing numbers to hear him. His fame as the great proponent of the Word of God and the Reformation spread beyond Worcester to the whole kingdom. The Spanish ambassador said that Latimer had made more heretics than Luther. In one rural diocese where the bishop favoured the old religion, a man was brought before the Bishop's Court charged with neglecting a saint's day ceremony. 'Latimer preaches that we should trust only in God's Word,' the man replied. 'And that we should not honour any saints, nor trust in any ceremonies of the church.'

While Latimer began his bishopric, the king dispatched commissioners to examine the spiritual condition of the monasteries. Henry knew that the monks had been the strongest supporters of papal authority and the loudest opponents of his divorce. He moved quickly to bring them to heel. Another reason for the king's interest was money; the English monasteries controlled a large proportion of the nation's land. Princes in Germany and the kings of Sweden and Denmark had already dissolved the monasteries in their realms and filled the royal coffers with the confiscated wealth. Henry VIII was desperate for money to pay for his fleet and army, and lavish households.

Latimer wanted to see the influence of the monks curtailed as well, for they fostered pilgrimages, superstitious practices and the cult of saints. Complaints about corruption and immorality in the monastic houses had been commonplace for years. To most Englishmen, a monk was a lazy lout.

Henry's agents found widespread corruption and debauchery in many of the abbeys. In several, they uncovered abbots keeping concubines and granting their children the use of monastic lands. Drunkenness and idleness abounded. The king's men shut down hundreds of small monasteries and convents and confiscated their properties. While Latimer favoured the closing of most monasteries, he did not support the grabbing of all their lands and property by the king and his rapacious noblemen. Latimer pleaded with the king's ministers to use the funds of the abbeys to endow churches and Christian schools and to help the needy. 'It could not be for the honour of the king,' Latimer said, 'to take away the rights of the poor.'

When Latimer learned that Henry had used an abbey to quarter his horses, he confronted the king at court, saying, 'Abbeys were ordained for the comfort of the poor. It is not decent that the king's horses should be kept in them, thereby diminishing the living of poor men.'

Afterwards, an angry courtier questioned Latimer: 'What do you have to do with the king's horses?'

'I spoke my conscience,' Latimer answered, 'as God's Word directed me.'

Latimer preached often before the king and his court, calling them to trust Christ and obey him. He bluntly preached against sins that were rampant in Henry's court: adultery, greed and injustice. Once after a sermon, a courtier confronted Latimer with King Henry standing nearby. He accused him of preaching 'seditious doctrine'. The king turned to Latimer and asked, 'What say you to that?'

'Sir,' Latimer replied to his accuser, 'what would you have me preach before the king? Would you have me preach nothing as concerning a king in the king's sermon?' Then Latimer turned to Henry and said, 'If your Grace allows me for a preacher, give me leave to discharge my conscience; give me leave to frame my doctrine according to my audience.' After the exchange, a few of Latimer's friends at court came to him with tears in their eyes and said, 'We think you will be locked in the Tower by nightfall.' The impetuous king did not begrudge his boldness, and Latimer continued to enjoy Henry's favour. 'The Lord directed the king's heart,' Latimer said later.

Although the king had promised in 1530 to commission a translation of the Bible into English, laws against owning a copy of the Bible in English had not been repealed. No real progress had been made to establish a translation team to produce the Scriptures in English. But in the summer of 1535, Archbishop Cranmer received for his approval a copy of Coverdale's Bible. Miles Coverdale (1488–1568) had been a Cambridge disciple of Robert Barnes, the fiery Cambridge reformer. Coverdale had assisted William Tyndale in Antwerp. Coverdale took the work of Tyndale and added to it his own translation of several books of the Old Testament which Tyndale had not completed before his arrest and execution. He had it printed in Europe without Tyndale's commentary notes, which had so offended the church's old guard. Cranmer declared it 'better than any other translation hitherto made.'

He sent it to Cromwell for the king's approval. Henry immediately granted a licence for it to be printed and distributed. He further decreed that the Bible should be placed in every church in the realm 'for every man that will to look and read thereon.' Finally, after several years of cajoling by Cranmer and Latimer, the king had approved an English Bible for use in the kingdom. The reformers believed that if the Word of God lay at the heart of the Church of England then reformation of doctrine and practices would be inevitable.

The reformers taught that the Bible was the ultimate authority. The enemies of the Reformation held to the doctrine enshrined later by the Council of Trent. 'We must receive with similar respect and equal piety the holy Scriptures and tradition.' Determined to protect the old order, Bishop Gardiner complained, 'No, you can prove nothing by the Scripture. Scripture is dead. It must have a lively expositor.'

In 1536, Henry accused his wife, Anne Boleyn, of infidelity and treason. Church officials led by Cranmer annulled the marriage. Henry ordered Anne beheaded. The next day, he married Jane Seymour. Anne Boleyn had been a friend of the Reformation. She supported Latimer in his court preaching and his bishopric. There is no record of Latimer's reaction to Anne's death. Did he accept unquestioningly Cromwell's explanation that Anne had committed adultery? Did he concur with Archbishop Cranmer's pronouncement that 'the marriage was utterly void and of no effect'? Did it severely test his loyalty to such a harsh and despotic king? There is no evidence that he spoke a word in Anne's defence.

In June 1536, the first Convocation since the Act of Supremacy was assembled. Cranmer chose Latimer to preach the opening sermon. Four years earlier, Latimer had stood before Convocation as an accused heretic. Now, as a member of the elite body of churchmen, he charged them to promote the teachings they had previously condemned.

'Brethren,' he said, 'I pray you examine well, whether our bishops and abbots, prelates and curates, have been hitherto faithful stewards or not... They preached to the people redemption and forgiveness of sins, purchased by money and devised by man, not redemption purchased by Christ.'

He chastised the bishops for extolling their traditions above the Word of God and banning the Scriptures in English. 'But all your care,' he told them, 'is that no layman should read it: being afraid lest they by reading should understand it and understanding learn to rebuke your slothfulness.'

Latimer called them to drop their opposition to conducting worship services in English. 'Shall we evermore speak Latin and not English, that the people may not know what is said and done?' he asked. He told them that one day God would say to them, 'I commanded each of you to feed my sheep with all industry and labour, but you earnestly feed yourselves, wallowing in delights and idleness. I commanded you to teach my commandments and not your fancies; and to seek my glory, but you teach your own traditions and seek your own glory and profit.'

He spoke against purgatory, calling it a 'pick purse' and argued that no emperor ever got more money through his taxes than the church did from promoting its power to relieve souls in purgatory through the sale of indulgences and masses for the dead. He decried 'images, pictures, relics and pilgrimages encouraged by the clergy to the deception of the ignorant... These worldlings pull down the lively faith and full confidence that men have in Christ,' Latimer said, 'and set up another faith of their own making.'

Latimer railed against the luxury of the bishops and abbots who used their wealth not to care for the needy but to feed their own pleasures. 'If they spy profit, gains, or lucre in anything,' Latimer proclaimed, 'be it never such a trifle, be it never so pernicious, they preach it to the people.' 'Therefore, my brethren,' Latimer said in closing, 'leave the love of your profit; study for the glory and profit of Christ... Feed tenderly, with all diligence, the flock of Christ. Preach truly the Word of God.'

The startled bishops had never been addressed like this before. No doubt many seethed, longing for the good old days when they could have burned Latimer at the stake for such words. Latimer's message before Convocation was printed and read throughout the kingdom and Europe. His words resonated with many commoners. They knew that in Latimer they had a champion who cared for them body and soul.

Regretfully, most of the bishops opposed Latimer's reforms. Instead of taking steps to root out corruption and superstition in the church, they dug in their heels. They promoted prayer to saints, venerating images and adamantly opposed having worship services in English.

Despite the resistance of the bishops, the Reformation was on the rise. Throughout the kingdom, people debated the teachings and the ceremonies of the church. Henry, like other monarchs of his age, believed that it was 'his charge from God' to have all his subjects embrace the same faith; so the king instructed Convocation to settle the issues surrounding the disputed doctrines and practices.

As Convocation deliberated, Latimer, Cranmer and Fox, the Bishop of Hereford, promoted evangelical doctrines from the Word of God. Bishop Stokesley led those who opposed changes in the Church of England. 'It was all a delusion,' Stokesley responded, 'to believe that there was no other Word of God but that which every sower and cobbler read in their mother tongue. There were many unwritten verities, mentioned by the old doctors of the church, received from the apostles, which were of equal authority with Scripture.'

'Do you think that we can steal out of the world again the light which every man sees?' Bishop Fox asked. 'Christ has so lightened the world at this time that the light of the gospel has put to flight all misty darkness... The laypeople now know the Holy Scriptures better than many of us.'

After many days of debate, it became apparent that the reformers and the conservative bishops could not agree. With

Convocation deadlocked, Henry took over. In consultation with the bishops, he wrote the Ten Articles. The articles represented a blending of the beliefs and practices of the Roman church and those of the evangelical faith.

The articles held that Christ's physical body and blood were contained in the elements of the eucharist. One article affirmed the doctrine of purgatory and the efficacy of prayers for souls in purgatory. Latimer argued with the king against purgatory. Latimer defended his position from the Bible and the teachings of the early church Fathers. He reminded the king that most of the monasteries were founded by wealthy noblemen to provide for perpetual prayers for their souls in purgatory. Since Henry had dissolved many of the monasteries his stand on the existence of purgatory appeared contradictory. 'What uncharitableness and cruelness to destroy monasteries, if purgatory be!' Latimer wrote. Henry remained unconvinced. However, the article on purgatory included a condemnation of the Roman practice of pardons from purgatory or the sale of masses which claim to 'deliver them from their pain and send them straight to heaven.'

Although the Ten Articles contained things that discouraged the reformers, they saw movement in the right direction. The articles kept many of the ceremonies and practices of the Roman church, but added: 'None of these ceremonies have power to remit sin.' The use of images continued to be encouraged in the churches, but priests were directed to warn the people against worshipping them.

More importantly, the Ten Articles included elements of the doctrine of justification through faith in Christ alone.

This was a great advance, since King Henry feared that if the people believed that salvation was God's free gift of grace earned completely by Christ, then any motivation for good works and morality disappeared. For several years, reformers had told Henry that when true faith took root in the heart, it bore fruit in good works. One of the articles stated: 'That neither our contrition and faith, nor any work can merit or deserve justification. The mercy and grace of the Father, promised freely for Christ's sake, and the merits of his blood and passion, are the only sufficient and worthy causes thereof.'

At this time, the theology of the English reformers was still maturing. They had not yet shined the light of God's Word on all the teachings of the church. In time, they would change their minds on more of the doctrines inherited from the Roman church.

Latimer and the other reforming bishops gladly signed the Ten Articles. They knew they had to exercise patience as they pressed the headstrong king for reform. 'The drop of rain makes the hole in the stone,' Latimer said, 'not by violence, but by often falling. Likewise a prince must be won little by little.'

After Convocation passed the Ten Articles, Cromwell persuaded Henry to issue injunctions to the clergy for implementing the articles. These directives pleased the reformers because they did a great deal to advance biblical Christianity in the kingdom. The king directed all bishops and priests to exhort parents to teach their children the Lord's Prayer and the Ten Commandments in English. He commanded the clergy to discourage pilgrimages and to teach that it was far better to clothe the poor than decorate images. The clergy were to study the Scriptures and pastor their flocks diligently. Best of all, he ordered a copy of the 'whole Bible of the largest volume in English' to be placed in every church within the year for congregants to read.

When the session of Convocation ended, Latimer was delighted to go home. He did not enjoy the work of Convocation with its endless debates and political manoeuvrings. As bishop, he also served in Parliament's House of Lords. These duties kept him in London for months at a time. 'For my part,' Latimer said, 'I would rather be the poor parson of poor Kington again, than to continue thus as Bishop of Worcester.'

When Latimer returned to his diocese he set to work explaining the Ten Articles to his clergy and preparing them to receive the Word of God in English. He directed the ministers to buy a copy of the Scriptures before the year was out. He told them to read at least a chapter a day and carefully examine its meaning. Latimer required them to say aloud in English the Lord's Prayer, the *Apostles' Creed*, and the Ten Commandments with the congregation every Sunday. He directed each priest to teach the children of his parish to read English. 'So that thereby,' Latimer wrote, 'they may the better learn how to believe, how to pray, and how to live to God's pleasure.'

Many people eagerly embraced the Bible in English as one dying of thirst receives a cup of cold water. As they read the Gospels for themselves they found Christ depicted not as an unapproachable and wrathful judge, but as a gracious Saviour bidding them, 'Come to me.'

Soon, all over England people went to their parish church to read the Scriptures in English or to hear laymen read them aloud. 'Many of us would flock about them to hear their reading,' one young man said later, 'to hear that glad sweet tidings of the gospel. This put me upon the thought of learning to read English so that I might read the New Testament myself.'

'Truly, we are much bound to God,' Latimer said in a sermon, 'that he has set out his will in our natural mother tongue, in English. So that now you may not only hear it, but also read it yourselves; which is a great comfort to every Christian heart... We are not in darkness. We have the Word of God; we know what his will is.'

By 1537, Henry had reigned for nearly thirty years and there was no male heir to the throne. The English people feared a return of civil war with rival houses fighting for the throne. The reformers were anxious that Henry have a male heir to carry on further reforms of the church. Therefore, Latimer and the reformers rejoiced at the birth of Prince Edward (1537–1553) in October 1537. Sadly, Queen Jane died a few days after giving birth. Soon Henry started searching for his fourth wife.

After the king's commissioners had dissolved the smaller abbeys, they turned their attention to the larger ones. Rather than risk a forced dissolution imposed by the royal commissioners, most of the priors and abbots surrendered their abbeys to the Crown in exchange for a generous pension. In the summer of 1538, while the king's commissioners proceeded to close the abbeys of the Midlands, Latimer again appealed to the government to take some of the wealth to support schools. As he had benefited from an education in a rural district, so he wanted the poor farmers' sons of the Midlands to enjoy the same opportunity. He requested that the resources of the abbeys of the Blackfriars and Greyfriars in Worcester be used to maintain a Christian school and repair the city walls and its strategic bridge over the River Severn. The king granted the friaries to the citizens of Worcester.

All told, the government dissolved nearly 2,000 monastic institutions in the kingdom. The king used a small amount of the monastic wealth to endow several grammar schools and a few colleges, but mostly he replenished his treasury with the booty. Most of the monastic lands were sold by the king's government to English aristocrats who clamoured for them. These noblemen often claimed that they would use part of the land to support a school or hospital or church. Men who preyed upon the monastic lands to expand their own wealth while making grand promises of benevolence frustrated Latimer. He wrote, 'I like not these honey-mouthed men when I see no acts nor deeds according to their words.'

Another potential source of wealth for the Crown could be found in the pilgrimage shrines. Their relics and wonder-working images had long been a highly profitable business for clerics and a great stumbling block for the people. The king wanted to strip the shrines of their gold and precious jewels. Latimer wanted to root out any impediment to the gospel. Despite the king's directives to the English clergy to curtail the superstition and corruption associated with pilgrimages, journeying to the holy sites remained popular. So Cromwell and Cranmer took steps to discredit the sacred images in the minds of the people.

In February 1538, the famous Rood of Boxley was brought to Paul's Cross in London. When the king's men dissolved Boxley Abbey in Kent, they yanked its famous 'rood' or crucifix from the wall of the abbey church. For ages, sick pilgrims had lain prostrate before it in hopes of a cure. The crucifix contained springs, wires and pulleys which made the head and the body move. The image had drawn large crowds of pilgrims, which became a source of wealth for the abbey. Warham, the Archbishop of Canterbury, once described Boxley as 'so holy a place where so many miracles are showed'.

Latimer was present at Paul's Cross when the workings of the Rood of Boxley were exposed to the people in a sermon. After the message, the rood was passed out for the crowd's inspection. They smashed it to bits. Another supposedly miraculous crucifix, which had become a centre of superstition, had also been brought to St Paul's. The people believed that a team of sixteen oxen could not move it. Hugh Latimer picked up the image with his bare hands and threw it out of the west door of St Paul's Cathedral.

Among the most famous and lucrative of the pilgrimage destinations in England was the shrine of Our Lady of Walsingham. Locals claimed that in the eleventh century the mother of Jesus appeared in a vision to a woman in Walsingham, a village in Norfolk. A nobleman built a chapel to house a small statue of Mary and a crystal vial said to contain breast milk from the Virgin Mary. Stories of miraculous healings and other blessings from Our Lady of Walsingham spread across the kingdom. For centuries it was the second most popular pilgrimage site in Britain, surpassed only by the shrine of Thomas Becket at Canterbury. English kings and queens paid homage to the Lady, including Henry VIII, who once walked barefoot for two miles to see the statue and honour the Virgin.

Latimer despised the Marian shrines because they kept the people from looking to Christ for salvation. Latimer's Cathedral at Worcester had a statue known as 'Our Lady of Worcester'. People came to the city on pilgrimage to give offerings, decorate the image and kiss it. In so doing, they believed that they would receive a blessing for their devotion. Latimer stripped it of its gems and layers of costly silks and linens. Like the apostle Paul's critics in Ephesus, one devotee of the Lady of Worcester stood before the bare statue in the cathedral and complained to a gathered crowd about Latimer's stand against images. 'The lucre and profits of this town is decayed through this,' he said.

Eventually, with Cromwell's permission, Latimer removed it from the church altogether, saying that he hoped it would turn the people from 'ladyness to godliness.' When Latimer learned that 'Our Lady of Walsingham' was being brought to London to be publicly burned, he sent the Worcester statue to Cromwell. 'She has been the devil's instrument to bring many, I fear, to eternal fire,' he wrote to the Chancellor. 'Now she with her old sister of Walsingham ... will make a jolly muster in Smithfield. They will not be all day in burning.'

Sadly, more than statues were burning at Smithfield. In April 1538, the friar John Forest was arrested for preaching against the Ten Articles and for telling penitents who came to him for confession that Henry was not the supreme head of the Church of England. Cranmer and Latimer urged Forest to recant, which he did. But before Forest was released from prison some friars met with him and convinced him to stand firm in the old faith. Forest withdrew his recantation. The king ordered his execution for heresy. Cromwell asked Latimer to preach at his burning. Latimer requested to preach from a platform near Forest so he could hear the message and recant. 'If he would yet with heart return to his abjuration,' Latimer wrote, 'I would wish his pardon.'

Forest did not adjure, and he perished in the flames.

A few months later, the heresy trial of John Lambert convened. Lambert came to faith in Christ through Thomas Bilney's witness. King Henry, with prodding from the conservative bishops, determined to punish anyone who denied the bodily presence of Christ in the sacrament. At this time Cranmer, Latimer and most English reformers held to the physical presence of Christ in the bread and wine. Lambert appealed to the king to hear his case. Henry considered himself a gifted theologian, and he led the questioning of Lambert. 'Is the sacrament of the altar the body of Christ or not?' Henry asked him.

Lambert ably defended the doctrine of the spiritual presence of Christ in the eucharist, but not a physical presence.

Cranmer and the other bishops debated with him and pleaded with him to change his views. But Lambert held his ground, and told the king, 'My soul I commend to God, but my body I submit wholly to your clemency.' 'If you commit yourself to my judgment,' Henry told him, 'you must die, for I will be no patron of heretics.' Lambert was burned at the stake at Smithfield. He died repeating the phrase, 'None but Christ; none but Christ.' In a few years, Latimer and Cranmer would embrace the very doctrine for which Lambert died.

The theological struggles between the bishops continued. Henry liked to balance the bishops who defended the old faith with evangelicals like Latimer. This kept both parties in the church from dominating and made them all look to the king for support. Reformers in Europe often chastised their English friends for progressing so slowly in changing the church. However, they had a difficult task working with a strong-willed and despotic monarch and an entrenched clergy fiercely resisting reform. Martin Bucer, the reformer of Strasbourg, wrote to Cranmer, praising him and the other reformers for having accomplished so much 'in the midst of so many impediments.'

Despite the growing support for the Reformation in England, many people bitterly opposed it. One man said, 'The Bishop of Canterbury is a knave bishop, a heretic and a Lollard as are the bishops of Worcester and Rochester. I hope to see them burned and would carry a faggot sixteen miles to help.'

Fragile health plagued Latimer throughout his ministry. As he pursued his many duties as Bishop of Worcester he grew exhausted and suffered frequently from lung infections, back and side pains, stones, colic, headaches and insomnia. He saw his illnesses as coming from the Lord's hand. 'I accept all as does please Almighty God,' he said.

As bishop, Latimer did not accumulate personal wealth as most prelates did. 'I could have more money in my purse,' he wrote Cromwell, 'if I would have followed the old trade in selling of sin and not doing my duty.'

While other bishops spent lavishly on decorating and furnishing their palaces, Latimer used the diocese's resources to provide for the needy and to assist some poorly compensated preachers and school teachers. 'I delight more to feed hungry bellies than to clothe dead walls,' he said.

After the king had broken with Rome, taken control of the English church, dissolved the monasteries, and stripped the shrines of their wealth, the usefulness of the reformers to his cause waned. Henry had always resisted much of what the reformers supported. He wanted a national church independent from Rome, yet rooted in the ceremonies and doctrines of the Roman faith. Therefore, in 1539 the king took steps to curtail church reforms. He sent a directive to all the bishops to order his subjects to embrace the old ceremonies of the church such as lighting candles and creeping to the cross on Good Friday. He called Parliament and Convocation into session to enforce religious unity.

With the support of conservative bishops and over the strong objections of Cranmer, Latimer and the other reformers, Henry persuaded Parliament to pass the act commonly known as the Six Articles. Those who opposed the law called it, 'the Bloody Statute' or 'the Whip with Six Cords'.

The Six Articles stated that:

- Christ was physically present in the bread and wine of the sacrament.
- It was not necessary for the people to receive both the bread and the wine.
- Clergy may not marry.
- Vows of celibacy must be kept.
- Private masses were beneficial.
- Penitents must confess their sins to a priest for absolution.

Harsh penalties awaited violators of the Six Articles. Anyone denying the physical presence in the eucharist was to be burned at the stake. Anyone who opposed any of the other articles could face imprisonment and loss of property. All existing marriages of priests, monks and nuns were declared dissolved. Cranmer quietly sent his wife back to her family in Germany. Since Latimer had never married, that article did not directly affect him; but he believed that forbidding ministers to marry was unbiblical.

At this time Latimer and Cranmer held to the physical presence of Christ in the eucharist, and still accepted the legitimacy of private masses. But Latimer did not believe that the Word of God supported the other articles, and he thought that there should be liberty of conscience regarding them. Latimer knew his duties as bishop would require him to conduct trials of those who did not hold to the Six Articles. If he was no longer a bishop, he would not have to enforce the articles which he opposed; but if he remained in his office he could help Cranmer advance the reformation of the church. Latimer struggled to know what to do.

Then Cromwell told him that the king wanted him to step down. So Latimer resigned as Bishop of Worcester. It was said that as Latimer took off his bishop's robes he skipped across the floor for joy, 'feeling his shoulders so light, and being discharged of such a heavy burden'.

5

The outcast restored

*Not everyone who says to me 'Lord, Lord,' will enter the
kingdom of heaven, but the one who does the will of my
Father who is in heaven*
(Matthew 7:21).

After Latimer resigned from his bishopric and no longer
supported the king's direction for the Church of England, Henry viewed him with suspicion. Latimer's friends
urged him to seek the king's favour and submit to the Six Articles, but he would not. The king ordered Latimer to be held
under house arrest in the home of the Bishop of Chichester.

When the Six Articles became law, many evangelical leaders
fled the country for the Protestant cities of Switzerland and
Germany, where they were influenced by men like Calvin,
Bucer and Melanchthon. One day they would bring what
they had learned back to England.

Not long after Latimer's house arrest began, Robert Barnes,
the fiery preacher and friend of Latimer from Cambridge,

suffered the king's wrath. Bishop Gardiner had preached a sermon against the Reformation at Paul's Cross. A few weeks later, Barnes preached an inflammatory sermon at Paul's Cross against the old faith and described himself and Gardiner as 'fighting cocks' battling with one another. Gardiner complained to the king. Barnes apologized and promised to read publicly a retraction. He did, but he went on to preach a strident evangelical message against traditionalist doctrines, so Henry sent him to the Tower of London.

Latimer defended his rash friend even though this exposed him to greater danger. Barnes wrote from the Tower, 'Many persons approve my statements, yet no one stands forward except Latimer.'

Although Latimer was forbidden to travel anywhere in the kingdom, friends could visit him. Latimer anxiously awaited news of the progress of the Reformation. In July 1540, he was grieved to learn that Barnes had been burned at the stake along with two other friends of Latimer. On the same day, Henry sought to balance the scales by executing three friars for their loyalty to the pope. 'I was desirous,' Latimer said later, 'to hear of execution ... I looked every day to be called to it myself.'

Meanwhile, the sordid saga of Henry VIII and his wives continued. In 1540, he married the German princess, Anne of Cleves, but immediately regretted it. Then Henry sent Cromwell to the Tower on accusations of treason. Cromwell's crime was most likely the fact that he had encouraged the king's marriage to Anne. With the arrest and later execution of Cromwell, the reformers lost a strong supporter at the head of the government. Henry's marriage was annulled. Soon Henry married his fifth wife, Katherine Howard. But after little more than a year of marriage, her ongoing sexual promiscuity was revealed. Parliament found her guilty of treason against the king. Henry ordered her execution.

In the summer of 1540, the king issued a general pardon for all who had offended against the Six Articles. Henry released Latimer from house arrest, but he forbade him to preach or to come within six miles of Oxford, Cambridge, London or the diocese of Worcester. He had no home and he could not preach. He stayed with friends and taught the Word of God to small gatherings. During this time he was injured by a falling tree, and his precarious health was weakened further.

The young reformer Thomas Becon told of meeting Latimer in the country manor of a mutual friend. Becon had been deeply moved by Latimer's preaching in Cambridge when he was a student there. He found his conversation with Latimer so spiritually uplifting that he felt as if he had been 'clean delivered from Egypt and quietly placed in the new glorious Jerusalem'.

Despite the preaching ban, the Holy Spirit was using Latimer to win souls to Christ. John Olde was one who put his trust in Jesus after talking with Latimer. Olde became a minister and Scripture translator. Years later, Olde wrote, 'I acknowledge from the bottom of my heart that Hugh Latimer was a right worthy instrument and minister of God. His most wholesome doctrine, godly life, and constant friendship toward me, God used to open to me the true Christian faith.'

Meanwhile, Bonner, the new Bishop of London, strictly enforced the Six Articles, by throwing hundreds into prison, casting a dark cloud over the evangelicals of London. Gardiner and Bonner did not want people reading the Bible aloud in the churches as had become a common practice throughout the land. In 1543, the advocates of the old religion persuaded Henry and Parliament to forbid anyone from publicly reading any part of the Bible in English unless they had been appointed by the king's government. Even Scripture reading in private was curtailed.

The Act permitted noblemen and landed gentry to read the Bible to their families, but the common people ('women, artificers, apprentices, journeymen, yeomen, husbandmen and labourers') were forbidden to read the Scriptures at all. During the same year, Henry proclaimed, 'Reading of the Holy Scripture is not so necessary for the laity that they be bound to read it, but as the Prince and the policy of the realm shall think convenient it may be tolerated or taken from them.'

As the enemies of reform gained influence with the king, they took steps to incriminate Cranmer before Henry. But the king would have nothing of it and continued to defend the Archbishop of Canterbury.

During this time Henry married his sixth and final wife, Catherine Parr, a devout supporter of the Reformation. She used her influence prudently to nudge Henry toward greater reforms. In 1544, the king mandated that all prayers in church should be spoken in English. Cranmer was the primary author of these prayers and they were the beginnings of what became the *Book of Common Prayer*.

In 1546, the last full year of Henry's reign, the Reformation suffered setbacks. Edward Crome, a reformer and friend of Latimer, had preached a sermon against purgatory. Crome was hauled before the Privy Council. Under questioning and threats, he recanted. Latimer had met often with Crome. So the Council interrogated Latimer about him and probed into Latimer's beliefs. He told them that he thought he would enjoy more rights under the Turks than under this Council. Latimer said, 'I desire to speak with his Majesty himself before I make further answers.'

They turned him over to the king, who threw Latimer in the Tower of London. There he daily awaited execution for a year and a half until the death of King Henry VIII.

At about the same time, Anne Askew, an outspoken evangelical and a friend of the queen's ladies at court was arrested for heresy. Bonner and the Mayor of London interrogated and tortured Anne, then cast her into the Tower. After two days of interrogation, she wrote, 'I was sore sick, thinking no less than to die; therefore I desired to speak with Master Latimer, but it would not be.' The authorities had no intention of permitting Askew the comfort of a conversation with her fellow prisoner, Hugh Latimer.

After Askew's death, Bishop Gardiner and the other proponents of the Roman faith tried to remove the influence of Henry's evangelical queen. Henry had complained in court about his wife 'instructing us' in religious conversation. 'Should I be taught by my wife in my old age?' the king asked aloud.

But when Gardiner and others took steps to undermine her, Henry stopped them in their tracks. The king removed Gardiner from the Privy Council. He placed supporters of the Reformation in charge of the oversight of his son Edward to run the government as regents of the boy king until he came of age. Henry VIII died a few days later.

In February 1547, when Henry's nine-year-old son was crowned King Edward VI in Westminster Abbey, his government declared a general amnesty. The Duke of Somerset, whom the Privy Council appointed to rule in Edward's name, was an evangelical. Somerset encouraged Cranmer to press forward with reforms. Hugh Latimer was released from the Tower. He went to live in Lambeth Palace with Archbishop Cranmer. Cranmer granted him licence to preach anywhere in the kingdom, lifting Henry's eight-year ban on his preaching. As the reformation of the Church of England accelerated, Cranmer was its chief author and Latimer its foremost preacher.

Parliament overturned Henry's Six Articles and abolished statutes against reading the English Scriptures. Ministers were permitted to marry. Through the influence of the Continental reformers, Cranmer and Latimer rejected the Roman doctrine of the physical presence of Christ in the bread and wine. They came to see that the real presence of Christ in the sacrament is not found physically in the bread that the priest holds, but spiritually in the hearts of believers who receive the elements by faith.

Under Cranmer's leadership, church services changed dramatically through the use of the *Book of Common Prayer*, a new liturgy for worship services in English. Now the people began to experience the Reformation of the church at first hand. During Henry's reign, worshippers continued to experience what they had for centuries. The people were passive, merely spectators of a ritual performed by a priest. The priest spent most of the service speaking Latin before an altar with his back to the people. The sermon, if there was one, was short. The priest alone received the wine from the cup. Most laypeople took communion just once a year at Easter; and when they did, they only received bread.

Suddenly, all that changed. Now the minister spoke English for the entire service, and the congregation participated with responses and prayers in English. The minister wore a simple black gown, not elaborate layers of clerical garb. The Scriptures were read, and expounded in a substantial sermon. At communion, the people received not only the bread, but also the wine which had been denied them for centuries. The bread and wine were no longer taught to be physical manifestations of Christ's body and blood; the Lord's Supper was a commemoration of Christ's sacrifice on the cross, and he was spiritually present to all who trusted in him. Gone were petitions for souls suffering in purgatory and so were prayers addressed to Mary and the saints. Gone were the ceremonies of lighting candles, smearing ashes, carrying palms and creeping to the cross.

Parliament petitioned Edward's government to restore Latimer as Bishop of Worcester. Nothing came of it; and it is likely that Latimer would have turned it down if it had been offered. He realized that his calling was preaching the Word of God, not administering a diocese. He often preached before the boy king and to large crowds at Paul's Cross. Wherever Latimer was scheduled to preach, the church could not contain the crowd that flocked to it. Once, when he preached in St Margaret's Church at Westminster, the throng pressed in so tightly that they left the pews broken in pieces.

The vast majority of priests within the Church of England were woefully uneducated in the Scriptures and largely incapable of producing scriptural sermons. Cranmer instituted the *Book of Homilies* (sermons written by himself, Latimer and others) to promote biblical Christianity in the church. The reformers knew that it was not enough to provide the Bible in English to the clergy and the people. Biblical truths had to be proclaimed from the pulpit. 'God's instrument of salvation is preaching,' Latimer said.

The homilies were 'to be declared and read by all parsons, vicars or curates every Sunday in their churches'. The sermons touched a variety of themes including the Word of God, justification by faith, and good works.

Edward's government used a heavy hand to impose the worship changes. Ministers were required to use the *Book of Common Prayer* on pain of imprisonment. When Bishops Gardiner and Bonner refused to implement the homilies in their dioceses, the Privy Council cast them into prison for a time. Eventually, they were stripped of their church offices.

In January 1548, Latimer preached at Paul's Cross a message from Christ's parable of the sower, entitled 'On the Plough'. In the sermon, he compared the work of a preacher to that of a ploughman. Latimer wanted the commoners, the ruling classes and the churchmen in the crowd to know what Christ expected of his ministers. Latimer told the crowd: 'He [the preacher] has a busy work to bring his parishioners to a faith that embraces Christ and trusts to his merits; a lively faith, a justifying faith, a faith that makes a man righteous, without respect of works … and then to confirm them in the same faith. Now casting them down with the law and with threatenings of God for sin. Now ridging them up again with the gospel and with the promises of God's favour. Now weeding them by telling them their faults and making them forsake sin. Now clotting them by breaking their stony hearts to make them soft hearts, and apt for doctrine to enter in. Now teaching them to know God rightly and to know their duty to God and their neighbours. Now exhorting them, when they know their duty, to do it diligently.'

Then Latimer criticized the bishops who preached just once a year or not at all. Instead, they enjoyed their privileges while lording it over the people. 'For the preaching of the Word of God to the people is called meat,' Latimer proclaimed. 'Scripture calls it meat; not strawberries that come but once a year and are soon gone. It is meat, it is not dainties. The people must have meat that is familiar, continual, and daily given to them to feed upon. Many make a strawberry of it, ministering it but once a year.'

'For ever since the prelates were made lords and nobles,' Latimer continued, 'the plough stands still; there is no work done, the people starve. They hawk, they hunt, they card, they dice … so that ploughing is set aside. By their lording and loitering, preaching and ploughing is clean gone.'

Latimer warned the people that although the bishops and priests might stand idle, there was one person who never did. 'And now I will ask a strange question,' he said. 'Who is the most diligent preacher and prelate in all England? I can tell you for I know him well. The most diligent preacher in all England is the devil! He is ever at his plough to devise many ways to deface and obscure God's glory. Where the devil has his plough going, there away with books and up with candles; away with Bibles and up with beads; away with the light of the gospel and up with the light of candles ... Down with Christ's cross and up with purgatory pick-purse.'

He closed his sermon on the plough by bringing his hearers back to the Saviour. 'Then let us trust upon his only death,' he said, 'and look for no other sacrifice. But as for our redemption, it is done already, it cannot be better. Christ has done that thing so well that it cannot be amended.'

Whenever he preached before Edward VI, a warm supporter of the Reformation, and his court, four times the number of lords and ladies came that could fit in the royal chapel. So he spoke from a pulpit built in the king's garden at Westminster Palace to accommodate the crowd. Latimer, no respecter of persons, preached against the injustice and corruption that was rampant in the government. He made many enemies. Even in the time of Edward, Latimer knew that he might pay for his words. He often told his friends, 'Preaching the gospel will cost me my life.'

Latimer's preaching was blunt and uncompromising. He preached the righteousness of Christ and Christ's command to live righteously. 'Convert, repent and amend', was his constant call. 'The goodness of God draws us to amend our lives.'

He made stark statements about those who claimed faith in Christ but bore no fruit. 'What shall be the end of all covetous persons?' Latimer asked in a sermon. 'Eternal damnation.' However, he always made clear the right understanding of the believer's good works. In a sermon on the Beatitudes he said: 'You must understand that all our works are imperfect; we cannot do them so perfectly as the law requires because of our flesh which ever hinders us. Why then is the kingdom of God called a reward? Because it is merited by Christ: for as touching our salvation and eternal life, it must be merited, but not by our own works, but only by the merits of our Saviour Christ. Therefore believe in him, trust him; it is he that merited heaven for us: yet for all that, every man shall be rewarded for his good works in everlasting life, but not with everlasting life... Yet God has such pleasure in such works that we do with a faithful heart that he promises to reward them in everlasting life.'

One of the first sermons that Latimer preached before Edward's court was on Christ's command to believers to make restitution to those against whom they had sinned. The court was full of people who had gained wealth by defrauding others. When Latimer informed the court that he would preach on restitution, one nobleman said, 'Restitution, why preach on restitution? Preach on contrition and let restitution alone. We could never make restitution.'

'Then,' Latimer said, 'if you will not make restitution, you shall go to the devil for it. Now choose either restitution or endless damnation.'

After the sermon, a man with a guilty conscience approached Latimer. He confessed that, under the direction of his former superior, he had deceived the king and defrauded the royal treasury of a large sum. Latimer advised him to contact his superior and make restitution. They paid back the money to the king's treasurer. The man who was so moved by Latimer's sermon was John Bradford. Bradford gave his heart to Christ and Latimer became his mentor. Through Latimer's encouragement, Bradford became a preacher and a leading reformer and a royal chaplain to Edward. Later, Bradford would share a prison cell with Latimer.

During Edward's reign, some used the doctrine that souls are saved by faith through grace and not by works as an excuse to disregard the commandments of God. One observer of Edward's courtiers wrote, 'Those very persons who wish to be, so to speak, most evangelical, imitate carnal licentiousness under the pretext of religion and liberty. Every kind of vice, alas, is rife among them.'

Latimer told his hearers that they served a holy God who was to be loved, feared and obeyed. He reminded them that a great day of judgement awaited everyone. 'Consider the matter, good people,' he preached, 'what a dangerous thing it is to fall into the hands of the Everlasting God. Leave falsehood: abhor it! Let us beware. Let us not displease him. Let us not be unthankful and unkind. Let us receive with all obedience and prayer the Word of God.'

Corruption infected many in the royal court. Government officials took bribes to bestow church offices. They gave church lands to their friends and family, crippling the traditional means of support for the clergy. Men received the income of benefices, but never darkened the doors of the churches for which they were responsible. Hundreds of churches in the kingdom had no resident minister to bring the people the Word of God. 'The sellers of offices show that they believe that there is neither hell nor heaven,' Latimer preached before the royal court. 'It is taken for a laughing matter.'

Many officials were notorious for their total disregard for justice for the poor and the powerless. In a court sermon Latimer described the case of a woman brought to trial for murdering her three children. But she had money and influential friends. She bribed the judge and was released. 'Where, at the same sessions,' Latimer said, 'another poor woman was hanged for stealing a few rags off a hedge that were not worth a crown.'

'Bribery is a princely kind of thieving,' Latimer preached to the king's court, 'waged by the rich, either to give sentence against the poor, or to put off the poor man's causes. My lords-judges, you should be more afraid of the poor widow than of a nobleman with all his friends and power... The greatest man in the realm cannot so hurt a judge as a poor widow... And how is that? Because God, the Judge of widows, the Father of widows and orphans, hears their cries. For their sakes he will hurt the judge be he never so high. He will for widows' sakes change realms, bring them into subjection, and pluck the judges' skins over their heads.' He wanted the courtiers to remember Christ in the midst of their luxury. 'Mix your pleasures with the remembrance of his bitter passion,' he told them.

Many of the common people viewed Latimer as their advocate. Whether he was staying in the home of a friend or residing with Cranmer at Lambeth Palace, poor people sought his help. 'I am no sooner in the garden,' Latimer said, 'but by and by there comes someone knocking at the gate, someone that desires that I will speak so that his matter might be heard.'

Latimer often appealed to government officials to redress the wrongs of the downtrodden folks who brought their complaints to him. No wonder the poor and the dispossessed saw Latimer as their champion and the ruling classes despised him and chafed under his preaching. 'They cannot be content to hear God's minister condemning their sin,' Latimer said of the avaricious members of the ruling class, 'though the sermon be never so good, though it be never so true.'

Those who did not like his sin-searching sermons told Latimer, 'You lack discretion.' They called him 'foolish and rash; a troublemaker in the realm'. 'I rejoice sometimes when my friends come and tell me that they find fault with my discretion,' Latimer said. 'I think it likely that the doctrine is true; for if they could find fault with the doctrine, they would not charge me with a lack of discretion, but they would charge me with my doctrine.'

Latimer was renowned for his blunt sermons to the powerful, but he proclaimed truth and exposed sin among country folk just as strongly. Once when he was preaching in a rural church, he crafted his message against greed with a homely example that they would understand and remember. 'I have known some that had a barren cow,' he said. 'They would fain have had a great deal of money for her. Therefore they go and take a calf of another cow and put it to this barren cow and so come to the market pretending that this cow has brought that calf. And so they sell their barren cow six or eight shillings dearer than they should have done. The man who bought the cow goes home. He has many children, and has no more cattle but this cow, and thinks he shall have some milk for his children... The other fellow who sold the cow, thinks himself a jolly fellow and a wise merchant... But I tell you, whoever you are, that if you act like that you shall do it of this price — you shall go to the devil, and there be hanged on the fiery gallows, world without end.'

Although Latimer's sermons were strong and passionate, he often used humour to make his point. Once when preaching about faith leading to godly living, he told a story of a man buying a horse from his friend. When the day of the purchase arrived, they argued about what had been the agreed-upon price. Eventually, they brought lawsuits against one another to court. 'The end result?' Latimer asked. 'The lawyers got twice the value of the horse.' In a sermon about the importance of hearing God's Word preached, he told the congregation of a lady in London who met one of her neighbours in the street. 'Mistress, where are you going?' the neighbour asked. 'I am going to the sermon at St Thomas's

Church,' the lady answered. 'I could not sleep all last night, and I am going there now. I never failed of a good nap there.'

During Edward's reign, the majority of the bishops did not favour the Reformation. However, when the opportunity arose to replace bishops, Cranmer petitioned Edward's government to install evangelicals. In 1550, Nicholas Ridley (c. 1500–1555), a brilliant Cambridge theologian and reformer, became the Bishop of London. He insisted on biblical preaching and he sought to root out superstition from the churches of London. Ridley was Cranmer's primary assistant in writing the Forty-Two Articles which set down the fundamental doctrines of the Christian faith for the Church of England. They stressed the Scriptures as the only infallible rule of faith and practice. The Articles included the Bible's central teachings on the Trinity, the person and work of Christ, sin, and good works. They stressed the sovereignty of God in saving sinners — salvation by faith alone, through grace alone, by Christ alone, for the glory of God alone. The Forty-Two Articles reflected a maturing evangelical faith informed by the Scriptures, and demonstrated the great progress made by the English reformers under Edward.

Ridley greatly admired the old reformer, Hugh Latimer. He once wrote to the Lord Protector: 'Master Latimer is a man appointed of God and endued with excellent gifts of grace to set forth God's Word to whom the King's Majesty and the whole realm is much bound, not only for his constant maintenance and defence of God's truth when papists and persecutions did assault the godly, but also for that now he preaches the gospel so purely and freely rebukes the worldly of his wickedness.'

Heresy trials were greatly curtailed during Edward's reign. No one was put to death for holding fast to the old faith, but a few poor souls were condemned to the flames. The reformers agreed with Roman Catholics that those who denied the Trinity should be punished, even burned. They had not yet reached the wisdom of Anne Askew, who was executed during King Henry's reign. She told Bishop Bonner, who condemned her to death, 'I have searched the Scriptures, yet I have never found either Christ or his apostles put anyone to death.'

After 1550, Latimer no longer preached for the royal court. During the last two years of Edward's reign, he often stayed with friends in the English countryside and preached in small churches. One place that Latimer visited frequently was the country estate of John Glover in Warwickshire. Like Bilney, Glover had despaired, fearing that he had committed the unpardonable sin. Latimer showed him the full forgiveness in Christ revealed in the Scriptures for believers, and Glover was restored to peace with God.

Latimer preached often in the great hall at Grimsthorpe, the country castle of the Duchess of Suffolk. As she grieved the loss of her two sons, who died in a plague of sweating sickness in 1551, Latimer's consolation and biblical wisdom lifted her spirits.

He spent his time in spiritual conversation, prayer and Bible study. His friend and assistant, the Swiss reformer, Augustine Bernher, described Latimer's routine. 'He preached for the most part every Sunday twice, not to speak of his diligence in his own private studies ... every morning ordinarily, winter and summer, about two o'clock in the morning, he was at his books most diligently; so careful with his heart to the preservation of the church and the good success of the gospel.'

Latimer would have gladly finished his remaining days this way, but a new regime bent on persecuting evangelicals prevented it.

6

The trial

Be strong and courageous. Do not fear or be in dread of
them, for it is the LORD your God who goes with you. He will
not leave you or forsake you
(Deuteronomy 31:6).

In the summer of 1553, King Edward died at the age of
15. Although the Reformation advanced under his
reign, many of his subjects turned against it because of the
injustice and avarice of the elite. Others, comfortable with
the old faith and its rituals, resented the changes in worship
and practice imposed upon them. Next in line to the throne
was Princess Mary (1516–1558), daughter of Henry and
Catherine of Aragon. Mary, a strident Roman Catholic,
had throughout Edward's reign refused to hear evangelical
preachers or attend a worship service in English. She went to
Latin mass in her private chapel. As his health deteriorated,
Edward worried that his half-sister would use her power to
eradicate the Reformation root and branch. Edward was not
the only evangelical concerned about Mary.

Lord Protector Northumberland (1501–1553) wanted to maintain his control of the government and to preserve the English Reformation. While Edward VI lay dying, he hatched a plot with his councillors to bypass Mary and Elizabeth as heirs to the throne. With the cooperation of Edward, they wrote a will declaring Lady Jane Grey (1537–1554), who was the great-niece of King Henry VIII and the daughter-in-law of Northumberland, heir to the throne. The leading officers of church and state, including Archbishop Cranmer and Bishop Ridley, signed the will and attempted to enforce it when Edward died.

Supporters of the Roman faith wanted Mary to be their queen. Many Protestants believed that Northumberland had committed treason by trying to put his daughter-in-law on the throne. There was widespread hatred of Northumberland and his friends, who had grabbed so much land and wealth during Edward's short reign. Crowds in London protested in favour of Mary's right to reign.

The plot to deny Mary the crown collapsed in less than two weeks. Thousands of evangelicals rallied to Mary as the rightful heir to the throne. She assured them that they had nothing to fear from her, promising not to overthrow the reformed faith in England. Before long, Northumberland, Lady Jane Grey, and most of the high officials of church and state who had supported them, including Archbishop Cranmer and Bishop Ridley, were cast into the Tower of London.

Despite her early claims to the contrary, Mary's goal was to restore the Church of England to the authority of the pope. She forbade anyone to preach in England unless granted a royal licence to do so. She installed Stephen Gardiner, a conservative bishop deposed and imprisoned during Edward's reign, as the Lord Chancellor. Under Mary's direction, Gardiner removed the evangelical bishops and replaced them with Roman Catholics. At Oxford and Cambridge, any college heads or fellows who supported the Reformation were expelled.

Soon Mary assembled a Parliament agreeable to her views. Politicians who had declared themselves evangelicals under Edward quickly proclaimed themselves followers of Rome. Parliament repealed all the laws concerning religion passed during King Edward's reign. Mary's government demanded the return of the Roman mass in every church under penalty of law. Out went the worship service in English and back came the mass in Latin. Out went the English Bible and back came images and holy water. Out went married ministers and back came priests and monks vowed to celibacy. Out went the wine for the people at communion and back came the eucharistic host to be adored as the physical body of Christ. Any minister who spoke against the queen's actions lost his position and was jailed.

Many reformers fled to Germany or Switzerland for safety, and some hid within the kingdom. Some accepted what the new government imposed upon them and bided their time until a change of regime would be more favourable to the evangelical cause. Others stood firm and suffered for their faith. Latimer was not surprised by the turn of events, nor did he despair. A year before Mary came to power he preached a message about faithful ministers. 'What thanks had they for their calling, for their labour?' Latimer said. 'Truly this — John the Baptist was beheaded; Christ was crucified; the apostles were killed: this was their reward for their labours. So all preachers shall look for no other reward.'

As Mary asserted her control in London, Latimer lived quietly in the English countryside. It had been years since he was a bishop, and he no longer played a role at court. Latimer had had nothing to do with the attempt to place Jane Grey on the throne. He still preached regularly, but he was an old man in poor health. However, Mary's government had no intention of leaving Latimer alone. He had done more than any other preacher to win hearts for the English Reformation and expose the abuses and false doctrines of the Roman church. To countless English evangelicals he remained their champion.

The queen's Privy Council ordered Latimer to appear before them. They sent a messenger to summon him to London. A friend warned Latimer of his impending arrest and pleaded with him to flee. Instead of escaping for his life, he packed his bag and waited for the queen's officer. Not long before, he had said in a sermon, 'Happy is he to whom it is given to suffer for God's holy Word's sake! It is the greatest promotion that a man can have in this world, to die for God's sake.'

When the man with the arrest warrant arrived, Latimer greeted him cheerfully, saying, 'My friend, you are a welcome messenger to me. And I want you and all the world to know that I go as willingly to London now, being called by my prince to render a reckoning of my doctrine, as ever I went to any place in the world.'

To Latimer's surprise, the queen's agent did not arrest him and bring him back to London. He simply informed Latimer that he was to go to London and report to the Privy Council. The queen's government may have hoped that Latimer would escape. They could then discredit him as a coward. Instead, he straight away headed for London. Latimer knew that he was probably going to his death. On his way as he passed through Smithfield, the usual place of public execution in London, he said, 'Smithfield has long groaned for me.'

Before the Council, Latimer firmly stood his ground while enduring the mockery and taunts of the Roman Catholics newly restored to power. With many threats, the Privy Council sent him to the Tower. 'He did behave himself stoutly in Christ's cause before the Council,' said his attendant, Bernher.

When Latimer arrived at the Tower, he met on the green one of the guards whom he recognized from the time that Henry VIII had cast him in the Tower. 'My old friend,' Latimer said to him, 'How do you do? I have come to be your neighbour again.' Latimer was thrown into a cold, damp cell. He maintained his sense of humour in the midst of trying conditions. In the dead of winter, the jailer denied him a fire to warm himself in his frigid cell. The bone-chilling air wracked his old body. 'They plan to burn me,' he told his jailer, 'but if I do not get a fire soon, I am likely to die of cold first.'

Hugh Latimer spent his days in prayer and careful study of the New Testament. He was not permitted to see his friends and fellow-prisoners, Thomas Cranmer and Nicholas Ridley. The Privy Council allowed each of the prisoners to have a servant attend him. The three reformers communicated with each other by writing notes which their attendants carried back and forth. It was clear to these leaders of the English Reformation that Mary intended to force the doctrines of the Roman church upon all Englishmen. In particular, anyone who denied the physical presence of the body of Christ in the eucharist would be burned at the stake for heresy. They knew that soon they would stand trial for their lives for their beliefs, and they wanted to defend the faith stoutly from the Word of God.

Ridley, the youngest and the best debater of the three, took the lead in preparing for the trial. He wrote down his reasons for rejecting the mass and transubstantiation. Ridley sent copies to Latimer and Cranmer, who returned them with comments. 'I have read over of late the New Testament three or four times deliberately,' Latimer wrote to Ridley. 'Yet I cannot find there transubstantiation, nor the sinews and marrow-bones of the mass.'

Although Ridley led in writing a defence of reformed doctrine, he looked to Latimer for strength and comfort. At the end of one of the arguments which he sent to Latimer in the Tower, Ridley wrote,

> I think I hear you saying to me, 'Trust not, my son, to these word-weapons, for the kingdom of God is not in words, but in power. And remember always the words of the Lord, "Do not imagine beforehand what and how you will speak, for it shall be given you even in that same hour, what you shall speak; for it is not you that speak, but the Spirit of your Father who speaks through you."'

Therefore, father, pray for me, that I may cast my whole care upon Him, and trust upon Him in all perils... Now, father, I pray you help me to buckle on this armour a little better; for you know the deepness of Satan, being an old soldier, and you have wrestled with him ere now, blessed be God that has ever aided you so well.

'Sir,' Latimer wrote back, 'you have well-buckled armour. I see not how it could be better. I thank you from the bottom of my heart for it; and you shall not lack my prayer, trusting that you do the same for me. For, indeed, *there* is the help.'

In another note to Ridley, Latimer wrote: 'Be of good cheer in the Lord... "God is faithful, who will not suffer us to be tempted above our strength." ... Happy are we. This is the greatest promotion that God gives in this world... not only to believe, but also to suffer.' 'Pray for me,' Latimer continued, 'for I am sometimes so fearful, that I would creep into a mouse hole. Sometimes God visits me again with his comfort. So he comes and goes, to teach me to feel and to know all my infirmity that I might give thanks to him.'

Meanwhile, Queen Mary married Prince Philip of Spain. He arrived with a fleet of ships and a very large entourage of officials, priests and monks. Long suspicious of Spain, the English people resented their presence and influence.

After a few months in the Tower, the reformers experienced an unexpected blessing. Captured rebels from Wyatt's failed rebellion to overthrow the queen swelled the number of inmates in the Tower. To make room, guards put Latimer, Cranmer and Ridley into the same small cell.

'God be thanked,' Latimer said. 'It was to our great joy and comfort.'

Soon their joy increased when John Bradford joined them. It was Bradford who years before was moved by Latimer's sermon to make restitution to the king. Ridley had ordained Bradford to the ministry and worked closely with him to reform the church during Edward's reign. The four men redeemed the time in prayer and preparation. Latimer said of their two months together, 'We did together read over the New Testament with great deliberation and painful study.'

The prisoners carefully searched the Scriptures to find any support for the Roman doctrines of Christ's bodily presence in the communion elements and the sacrifice of the mass. Latimer testified later at his trial, 'We could find no other presence, but a spiritual presence; nor that the mass was any sacrifice for sins. But in that heavenly book it appeared that the sacrifice which Christ Jesus the Redeemer did upon the cross was perfect, holy, and good. God, the heavenly Father, required no other sacrifice; but was pacified with that omnisufficient and most painful sacrifice of that sweet slain Lamb, Christ our Lord, for our sins.'

In the meantime, Parliament passed decrees forcing the people to attend mass under penalty of fine or imprisonment. The queen sent representatives to the pope to seek his forgiveness for England's rebellion against the Roman church. The pope granted the English nation absolution for their sins, and sent Cardinal Pole to England to reassert Rome's authority over the English church.

In March 1554, after the reformers had endured seven months in the Tower, the Privy Council ordered Latimer, Cranmer and Ridley to stand trial at Oxford University. They said their farewells to Bradford as guards led them away. Two days later, they were cast into Bocardo, Oxford's prison on the northern wall of the city. Soon the men were jailed in separate locations to prevent them communicating with each other.

Oxford University took the lead in throwing off the Reformation. Evangelical professors lost their positions. Students who refused to embrace the doctrines of Rome were whipped and threatened with expulsion.

Church officials chose a panel of the ablest theologians of the Roman faith from Oxford and Cambridge to dispute with the three well-known leaders of the English Reformation. They hoped to expose their views as heresy. And if, by chance, they could get one or all of them to recant, it would deliver a serious blow to the evangelical cause. All Oxford buzzed with anticipation of the coming trial.

They held the trial in St Mary the Virgin, the university church, a stately stone structure built in the thirteenth century with a high tower on the south side. The church sat in the heart of Oxford, surrounded by colleges. It was the scene of the largest religious and academic gatherings of the university. The trial opened with a grand procession. In front, an official carried an ornate crucifix followed by a choir and the scarlet-robed regents and doctors of the universities, leading in tow a great throng of students.

The commissioners sat in front of the altar. Students and townspeople packed every corner of the church.

The commission brought the prisoners in separately to argue alone against more than twenty of the kingdom's leading traditionalist theologians. The commission demanded that each man affirm or deny three articles of teaching regarding the physical presence of the body of Christ in the sacrament and the sacrifice of the mass. They examined Cranmer first and Ridley appeared after him. Both of the reformers rejected the articles.

Then Latimer was brought before the robed dignitaries. He wore a frayed coat, his spectacles hung around his neck by a string and he walked with the use of a cane. After he denied the doctrine of transubstantiation and the mass, Latimer held up his New Testament and said, 'I have read it over carefully seven times since coming to prison and I could not find the mass in it, neither the marrow-bones or sinews of the same.'

Dr Weston, Dean of Westminster and the chief commissioner, rose red-faced and declared, 'I will make you grant that the mass has both marrow-bones and sinews in the New Testament.' 'That you will never do,' Latimer replied.

The commission set Latimer's trial for Wednesday, and ordered guards to take him away. He had three days to prepare his defence.

On Monday and Tuesday, Cranmer and Ridley defended their beliefs from the Scriptures and the writings of the

Church Fathers. On Wednesday morning, 18 April 1554, a bailiff led Hugh Latimer to a crowded room in one of the colleges to stand trial. He was ill, and felt faint. 'Men and brethren,' Weston began, 'we are come together this day, by the help of God, to vanquish the strength of the arguments and dispersed opinions of adversaries against the truth of the real presence of the Lord's body in the sacrament.'

Latimer asked permission to read his answers to the articles which he had carefully written over the last three days. They refused. The commissioners demanded that he dispute his points with them. 'Disputation requires a good memory,' Latimer said. 'My memory is gone clean, and marvellously weakened, and never the better for the prison.'

Refusing to retreat one inch from his beliefs, Latimer said that Christ's physical presence was not in the bread and wine. 'There is no other presence of Christ required than a spiritual presence,' he said, 'and this presence is sufficient for a Christian man by which we abide in Christ and Christ abides in us, to the obtaining of eternal life, if we persevere in the true gospel.'

Latimer denied that in the mass the priest offered up Christ as a sacrifice. 'Christ offered himself for us in his own person,' Latimer proclaimed, 'once for all and never again to be done. You have no authority in God's book to offer up a Redeemer; we have an advocate with God the Father, Jesus Christ the righteous one; who once offered himself for us long ago.'

A commissioner told him that he committed treason because he refused to obey his rulers. Latimer acknowledged that Christians were called to obey the government. But he added, 'so long as they do not command things against the manifest truth. But now they do; therefore we must say with Peter and John, "We must obey God before man."'

Latimer scolded the commission for neglecting to teach the people from the Scriptures, and for holding worship services in Latin. 'You should preach the benefit of Christ's path to the people,' Latimer declared. 'Instead you speak to the wall in a foreign tongue.'

For three hours the commissioners interrogated him. Often, Latimer's answers were interrupted by laughter, jeers and insults.

'I have spoken in my time before two kings,' Latimer said, 'more than one, two, or three hours together without interruption: but now, I could not be suffered to declare my mind before you, without revilings, rebukes and taunts such as I had not felt the like in such an audience all my life long.'

Again and again they tried to argue with Latimer from the writings of church authorities. But he insisted that Scripture was the final authority. To Latimer the great question was not: What did Augustine or Ambrose or Hilary write? But rather, is it written in the Word of God?

One commissioner said, 'Then you are not of Chrysostom's faith, nor of St Augustine's faith.'

'I have said,' Latimer replied, 'when they say well, and bring the Scripture for them, I am of their faith.'

Latimer ended his written statement with these words: 'I will stand, with God's help, to the fire... If I could grant to the queen's proceedings... I would rather live than die; but seeing they are directly against God's Word, I will obey God more than man, and so embrace the stake.'

Weston said that Latimer got his doctrine from a few runaway apostates from Germany. He called the reformers, 'fling-brains', 'light-heads' and 'apes'. Weston warned him that he would think differently 'when a faggot is in your beard. But,' he added, 'the queen's grace is merciful, if you will turn.'

'You have no hope to turn me,' Latimer answered. 'I pray for the queen daily from the bottom of my heart that she may turn from this religion.'

The commission dismissed Latimer and retired to render a verdict. A bailiff led Latimer away. He knew that the verdict was a foregone conclusion. Soon he would be burned alive.

7

The stake

In the world you will have tribulation. But take heart;
I have overcome the world
(John 16:33).

Two days after the commission finished questioning the reformers, Latimer, Ridley, and Cranmer stood together before the commissioners in St Mary's Church. They refused one last chance to recant. The commission condemned them as heretics, and sent them back to their separate places of incarceration. The following day, the commissioners held a mass in St Mary's. Then they left the church in a great procession through Oxford with Weston lifting high the sacramental host. Onlookers knelt in adoration as it passed by. A guard brought Latimer outside to see the procession. Latimer thought that he was being led to the stake. When he realized the purpose of the procession, he turned away, unwilling to watch the spectacle.

The end was not to come so quickly. Queen Mary waited to burn the heretics until the pope's rule over the English church was restored. Month after month the condemned reformers awaited their fate. Their bold stands at their trials had encouraged evangelicals throughout the kingdom. One jailed preacher wrote to them: 'England has had but a few learned bishops that would stick to Christ even unto the fire... I cannot utter with pen how I rejoice in my heart for you three captains in the lead under Christ's cross and banner.'

Death by burning was a gruesome affair. Rainy English weather often dampened the wood and kindling, prolonging the time for the fire to do its work. A victim could quickly suffocate from smoke or might linger for hours in agony. Often, the authorities would permit a friend of the condemned to place a satchel of gunpowder around his neck to speed death. The three condemned men had plenty of time to imagine the coming pains. A number of reformers recanted rather than face the stake. Latimer wrote to Ridley, 'Fear of death persuades a great number. Be well aware of that argument.' At another time he said, 'This now is a comfortable thing that we know that Christ has overcome death; and not for himself, but for us, for our sake. So that when we believe in Christ, death shall not hurt us, for it has lost its strength and power.'

This did not mean that Christ's victory over death removed death's trial for believers. 'Christ our Saviour has killed our death,' Latimer said. 'Notwithstanding, death has bitter potions, but what then? As soon as death has done his office, we are at liberty and have escaped all peril.'

Although no members of the university faculties of Oxford or Cambridge expressed their support, the condemned men received notes of encouragement and aid from faithful believers. A widow in London had sent them aid in the Tower and at Oxford. Latimer sent her a short note of thanks: 'If the gift of a pot of water shall not be in oblivion with God, how can God forget your manifold and bountiful gifts, when he shall say to you, "I was in prison and you visited me"? God grant us all to do and suffer while we are here as may be his will and pleasure.'

Latimer's attendant, Bernher, adept and daring at smuggling letters in and out, kept the three men in touch with each other and the outside world. Through Bernher, they exchanged letters with Bradford and other reformers imprisoned and free who sought their counsel. 'Blessed be God,' Ridley wrote to Bradford, 'we are merry in God; and all our care is, by God's grace, to please and serve him.'

In prison, Latimer was grateful for extended times of prayer. Throughout his ministry he had emphasized the importance of prayer. 'But what makes our prayers acceptable to God?' Latimer asked and answered in a sermon. 'It lies not in our own power; we must have it by another means. How does our prayer please God? Prayer pleases God because Christ pleases God. When we pray, we come to him in the confidence of Christ's merits. They shall be heard for Christ's sake. Yea, Christ will offer them up for us.'

In his cell, Latimer knelt in prayer for so long that he could not rise to his feet without assistance. 'Prayer is our only remedy, to fetch help at his hands,' he said. Latimer prayed aloud, often in tears. He prayed for many things, but Bernher said that he returned to three petitions over again.

First, he asked the Lord for the courage to be true to Christ unto death. Second, he prayed that God would once again pour out his Spirit upon England. Third, he prayed that Princess Elizabeth might come to the throne soon and rule righteously.

By the end of 1554, Mary's government had been reconciled with the Church of Rome and the stage was set for the execution of the reformers. On 4 February 1555, John Rogers, a chaplain of Ridley's at St Paul's Cathedral, died valiantly at the stake for Christ. Many others soon followed. As heresy trials proliferated across England, the presiding bishops found to their irritation the defendants quoting from the sermons of Latimer and the writings of Cranmer, Ridley, Bradford and others.

The authorities in Oxford tried to keep the three condemned men ignorant of outside events, but word slipped through. In July 1555, they learned that their dear friend, John Bradford, had been burned at the stake in Smithfield. Bradford had called out before the flames engulfed him: 'O England, repent of thy sins!'

Hugh Latimer penned a final letter to encourage believers to press on in the midst of persecution. 'Read from the first of Genesis to the Apocalypse,' he wrote, 'and tell me whether any of the saints in the Old Testament found any fairer ways than we now find, whether any of the apostles and evangelists found any other way to the city whereunto we travel than by many tribulations... Here is not our home; let us therefore always have before our eyes that heavenly Jerusalem, and the way thereunto is persecution.'

Ridley continued to look to Latimer for strength. 'I do think,' Ridley wrote, 'that the Lord has placed old father Latimer to be his standard-bearer in our age and country against his mortal foe, antichrist.'

In late September 1555, Latimer and Ridley stood before a court of three bishops acting on behalf of the pope. They came to Oxford to confirm the guilty verdict declared by the commission a year and a half before. They gave the reformers one last opportunity to recant. They first questioned Ridley, while Latimer stood and waited in a cold passageway. When finally summoned, Latimer entered with his hat in hand, wearing a cap with two broad flaps buttoned under his chin. He wore a threadbare robe secured to his body by a leather belt. His well-worn New Testament dangled from his belt by a long string. His spectacles hung from a chain around his neck.

'Master Latimer,' said the Bishop of Lincoln, 'I and my lords here have a commission from the pope's holiness to examine you upon your opinions which you have affirmed and obstinately defend.' He charged Latimer to flee his errors and return like a lost sheep to the fold of the Church of Rome. 'For outside the unity of the church,' he added, 'there is no salvation and in the church there can be no error.'

Latimer slowly unbuttoned and removed his cap. The bishop warned him that if he did not recant, he would be cut off from the church like a 'rotten member' and turned over to the civil government for execution. 'Therefore, Master Latimer,' the bishop concluded, 'for God's love consider your position; remember you are a learned man; you have taken degrees, borne the office of a bishop; remember you are an old man; spare your body, accelerate not your death, and specially remember your soul's health.'

'Your Lordship exhorted me to come to the unity of the church,' Latimer said. 'I confess a catholic church, spread throughout all the world and apart from that church no man can be saved. But I know perfectly by God's Word that this church is in all the world, and has not its foundation in Rome only, as you say.'

Latimer argued that popes and bishops had often directed the church on the basis of their own ideas not the Scriptures. All church authority must be, he said, 'according to the Word and law of God, and not after man's own will and imaginations and fantasies.'

Soon the Bishop of Lincoln cut off the discussion. 'We came not to dispute with Master Latimer,' he said, 'but to take his answers to the articles.'

He proceeded to read the articles to which Latimer must answer. Latimer stood to protest that by answering their questions, he did not thereby acknowledge Rome's authority. He insisted that he was the subject of the English Crown and not the pope.

'We object to thee, Hugh Latimer,' the Bishop of Lincoln read aloud, 'that thou in this high University of Oxford, in April, 1554, have openly defended that the true and natural body of Christ, after the consecration of the priest, is not really present in the sacrament of the altar.'

'Every man, by receiving bodily that bread and wine,' Latimer answered, 'spiritually receives the body and blood of Christ, and is made a partaker thereby of the merits of Christ's passion. But I deny that the body and blood of Christ is in such sort in the sacrament as you would have it ... the bread is still bread, and the wine is still wine. For Christ himself calls it bread, St Paul calls it bread, the doctors confess the same, and the nature of a sacrament confirms the same.'

The bishop then asked Latimer if he still denied the church's teaching that in the mass a sacrifice is offered for the living and the dead. 'No, my Lord,' Latimer responded, 'Christ made one perfect sacrifice for the whole world; neither can any man offer him again, neither can the priest offer up Christ again for the sins of man, which he took away by offering himself once for all.'

The commissioners closed the hearing and told Latimer that they would give him one more day to reconsider his answers. 'No, my lords,' Latimer said, 'I beseech you to do with me now as it shall please your lordships. My mind is made up. I pray you not to trouble me again tomorrow.'

'We trust God will work with you before tomorrow,' the Bishop of Lincoln replied. 'You must appear again tomorrow, at eight o'clock in St Mary's Church.'

The next morning the presiding bishops sat on a raised platform in the chancel of St Mary's. An overflow crowd packed the church. Townspeople, students, professors and many from the surrounding countryside came to watch the conclusion of the great trial. Evangelicals wanted to see the steadfast faith of their heroes. Roman Catholics hoped to witness their just punishment or hear them recant their errors. Ridley was called first. He would not deny his beliefs. The commission condemned him and consigned him to the mayor for execution.

Then a bailiff led Latimer into the church. The aged reformer entered with an old felt hat tucked under his elbow. His back ached from having been jostled by the crowds who thronged the church. The bishops asked Latimer to respond one more time to the questions they had asked him the day before.

Latimer refused to change his opinions, and argued that his teaching was not contrary to the Word of God. The bishops declared Latimer a heretic, excommunicated him and handed him over to the civil authorities to be consigned to the flames.

Two weeks later, a great crowd gathered just outside the north wall of Oxford across from Balliol College to watch the execution. Workers drove a large iron stake in the ground and stacked bundles of dry sticks and twigs. On a large platform erected for the occasion sat the mayor, city officials and the heads of the colleges. Soldiers armed with pikes kept back the crowd. When all was ready, guards walked Latimer and Ridley through the streets of Oxford to the stake.

When they met at the stake, the two men smiled and embraced. They had not been together for a year and a half. 'Be of good heart, brother,' Ridley said, 'for God will either assuage the fury of the flame or else strengthen us to abide it.'

.

The condemned men knelt in the dirt and prayed. They arose and talked together until a guard ordered silence. A priest preached a warning to the people not to follow Latimer and Ridley into heresy. He condemned the men to the fires of hell if they refused to recant. When the sermon ended, Ridley asked, 'May we say a few words to the people?'

'No,' shouted the vice-chancellor, 'you may speak only to recant your errors.' 'Well then,' said Ridley, 'I commit our cause to Almighty God, who shall fairly judge all.' Latimer added, 'There is nothing hid, but it shall be revealed.'

Guards commanded them to get ready. After the reformers removed their coats and hats, Ridley prayed. 'Oh, heavenly Father, I give to you most hearty thanks, for you called me to be a professor of you, even unto death. I beseech you, Lord God, take mercy upon this realm of England, and deliver her from all her enemies.'

Then a bailiff stood Ridley and Latimer back to back against the stake and tightly wrapped a thick iron chain around their waists. Cranmer's jailer led him to the gatehouse tower of Bocardo to watch his two friends die. Ridley's brother-in-law stepped forward to tie a bag of gunpowder around his neck to speed his death in the flames. 'And do you have any for my brother?' Ridley asked. 'Yes, I do,' he said, and he gave a bag to Latimer.

Guards piled bundles of sticks waist high around the reformers. As they set fire to it, Latimer said, 'Be of good comfort, Master Ridley, and play the man. We shall this day light such a candle, by God's grace in England, as I trust shall never be put out.'

As the flames leapt up, Ridley cried in a loud voice, 'Lord, receive my spirit.' And Latimer prayed, 'O Father of heaven, receive my soul.'

The fire rapidly overwhelmed Latimer, and he died quickly. Ridley suffered many minutes of excruciating pain. 'Lord have mercy on me,' he prayed. Finally, the flames exploded the gunpowder, and his body drooped over the chain.

Cranmer, watching from the tower of the jail, wept. Many spectators cried, overwhelmed with pity at the gruesome scene. One man in the crowd was Julius Palmer, a Fellow of Magdalene College and bitter enemy of the reformers. During King Edward's time, Palmer said that none of the preachers of the Reformation 'would stand to death for their religion'. As Mary began to burn evangelicals at the stake, Palmer marvelled at the reports of their courage and zeal. Out of curiosity, he went to see the execution of the famous bishops. The Lord used the sight to open his eyes. After returning from the stake he told his friends, 'O raging cruelty! O tyranny — more than barbarous!' From that day forward he spent his time praying, studying the Scriptures and reading the reformers' books. He became an evangelical preacher, and was burned alive for his faith.

Shortly after their deaths, the prison writings and letters of Latimer and Ridley were published. The story of their steadfast faith at the stake swept across England, lifting the spirits and stiffening the spines of evangelicals throughout the kingdom. Queen Mary's persecution of the reformers and her submission of the English church to papal rule did not have the desired effect. The Spanish ambassador wrote during Mary's reign, 'I am told not a third of the people who usually go to church are now attending.'

Mary died childless three years later, and her half-sister Elizabeth, who favoured the reformed faith, came to the throne. Soon the biblical faith and the English Scriptures for which Latimer and the other reformers had fought so long and hard were restored to the Church of England.

Summary

Hugh Latimer was a warm-hearted lover of the poor of soul and poor of body. His straightforward, honest, and biblical preaching brought the gospel of Jesus Christ to thousands upon thousands of his countrymen. Through thirty years of ministry, his voice was the clearest and most influential in England for the great truths of the Reformation. Latimer proclaimed that salvation rested in Christ alone, through grace alone, by faith alone, to the glory of God alone, and that the Scripture alone was the Christian's authority.

Apart from Tyndale and the other translators of the Scriptures, Latimer and his friend Cranmer were the greatest champions of the English Scriptures. Latimer was the foremost preacher of the English Reformation, and his preaching set the standard for generations of English-speaking preachers to follow. His faith in Christ while facing death at the stake continues to inspire Christians nearly five centuries later.

Bibliography

Chadwick, Owen. *The Reformation.* Harmondsworth: Penguin Books, 1964.

Darby, Harold S. *Hugh Latimer.* London: Epworth Press, 1953.

Demaus, Robert. *Hugh Latimer, a Biography.* London: Religious Tract Society, 1881.

Dickens, A. G. *The English Reformation.* New York: Schocken Books, 1964.

Edwards, Brian H. *God's Outlaw: The Story of William Tyndale and the English Bible.* Darlington: Evangelical Press, 1976.

Foxe, John. *The Acts and Monuments.* Fourth edition, edited by J. Pratt. 8 vols. London: Religious Tract Society, 1877.

Latimer, Hugh. *The Remains of Hugh Latimer, Sometime Bishop of Worcester, Martyr, 1555*. Edited by George Corrie. Cambridge: The Parker Society, 1845.

Latimer, Hugh. *The Sermons of Hugh Latimer, Sometime Bishop of Worcester, Martyr, 1555*. Edited by George Corrie. Cambridge: The Parker Society, 1844.

MacCulloch, Diarmaid. *Thomas Cranmer: A Life*. New Haven: Yale University Press, 1996.

Merle d'Aubigné, J. H. *The Reformation in England*. 1853; reprinted, Edinburgh: Banner of Truth, 1962.

Moorman, John R. H. *History of the Church in England*. Third edition. London: A. C. Black, 1973.

Ridley, Jasper G. *Nicholas Ridley: a Biography*. London: Longmans, Green and Co., 1957.

Ridley, Nicholas. *The Works of Nicholas Ridley, D.D. Sometime Lord Bishop of London, Martyr, 1555*. Edited by Henry Christmas. Cambridge: The Parker Society, 1843.